For
because I am as excited
about your baby as I am
about my own!

with great love,
Christi

Chosen Children

Chosen Children

Compiled by
Muriel B. Dennis

Introduction by
C. Everett Koop, M.D.

GOOD NEWS PUBLISHERS
Westchester, Illinois 60153

To those special Chosen Children that have enlarged my life and who were brought into our family by Lane and Ebeth, Cal and Georgina, Elmer and Vi

Contents

Introduction

When I began the practice of pediatric surgery more than thirty years ago, I frequently carried out surgical procedures on children through an adoption agency in Philadelphia. I was greatly impressed by the motto that strung along the top of their letterhead. It said: "There is a homeless Lutheran child for every childless Lutheran home." The situation is much changed today. There are thousands upon thousands of childless homes waiting expectantly for a homeless child to be given them to rear. Alas, since we are killing over a million unborn children each year in the United States, most of these childless homes will never have the privilege of raising a child.

Back in those early days when I dealt with many adoption agencies relative to the care of their children requiring surgery, I was always impressed with the families who took a handicapped child because it seemed a special act of love on the part of the family and a special kind of good fortune for the child. I watched many of those handicapped youngsters grow up in their adoptive families and saw the blessing that a handicap brings to a family even as it so frequently does to families who have a natural born handicapped child. With the great scarcity of babies for adoption now, adoptive parents are looking for children of different racial color, children of ethnic backgrounds far different from their own, and yes, indeed, even handicapped children, some of whose handicaps are staggering as one contemplates the special care and love that will be necessary to see the adoptive process through to the end.

One of my patients, himself handicapped, has five or six normal siblings. Yet his parents found that raising him was so rewarding that they have changed their entire way of life, bought a farm, and have adopted six handicapped children.

This volume, *Chosen Children,* recounts in remarkable anecdotal fashion the trials and tribulations as well as the joys and triumphs of adopting a child who is different. It also provides great Christian insight into the whole adoptive process regardless of the status of the adoptive youngster.

Not every situation that will confront the adoptive family with a special child will be considered here, but the basic building blocks from which can be manufactured a family relationship based upon Christian love and understanding as well as guided by the sovereignty of God are complete.

When I was asked to write an introduction to this book, I thought it was because someone knew that I had special qualifications for the task. I was the father of four children, I had lost one of my natural born children in what the world calls an accident, my wife and I had taken a nine-year-old girl who was an orphan, I have spent my professional life with children and, finally, my particular interest has been the rehabilitation of the handicapped. So, I agreed that I was probably qualified to write an introduction and rather smugly thought I would learn little or nothing by reading this book. Such was not the case.

I did learn on the basis of my "qualifications" that the stories here are real, that they ring true, and that the way in which these parents have weathered their storms can be taken at face value as examples and guidelines for others to follow.

One of the qualifications I forgot to mention was that I also founded an adoption agency in the city of Philadelphia a number of years ago; therefore, I have been seen first hand the kinds of problems presented by the subject matter of this book as well as by the unwed mother, the single parent, and the general lack of Christian compassion for the girl who finds herself in one of these situations.

I witnessed a heartwarming situation not long ago in my practice. An unmarried pregnant woman had joined a very conservative independent Christian church when she realized she was pregnant, thinking that she would find there all the Christian love and support she needed. When the child was born, it had a very visible handicap and one very difficult for parents to live with for the four or five years it takes to be corrected either by nature or surgery. I was fearful that the unfortunate girl would find the Christian environment she sought more hostile than friendly only because I have often seen that happen in similar situations. However, to my surprise and delight this church surrounded that young woman and her child with love and attention and provided baby-sitting arrangements for the child so the mother could continue her teaching job. The whole affair became a beautiful witness to Christian love, compassion and understanding at a time when I least expected it. I would hope that this book might serve a similar purpose. It certainly tells of the situations as they are. It does not make adoption an easy thing nor does it make adoption of an ususual child any less real a problem than it actually is. Yet, it is an example of Christian love, of Christian fortitude, and of the kind of social action by Christians that we talk about more than we see.

I would hope further that it might be the beginning of other publications that seek alternatives. In a sense, this book provides an alternative to the near impossibility of adopting a normal cherubic youngster as was once the case. Perhaps now someone will deal with the alternatives to abortion so that pregnant women in their fright, uncertainty and despair can turn to the Christian community for any one of a number of alternatives rather to destroy a developing child before it is born.

There is something for almost everyone here, not just those who might be wondering about adoption. Especially for those who like chapter and verse to prove a point, *The Christian Meaning of Adoption* and *Delights and Dilemmas in Caring for the Fatherless* are beautiful examples of going back to the Word of God to solve the everyday problems that adoption might present to the adoptive family.

C. Everett Koop, M.D., Sc.D.

Surgeon-in-Chief, The Children's
Hospital of Philadelphia

Professor of Pediatric Surgery
University of Pennsylvania
School of Medicine

Prologue / The Christian Meaning of Adoption

Lane T. Dennis

A few weeks ago as I walked in the door from work, our little seven-year-old daughter, Jenay, came running up to me enthusiastically asking, "Guess what happened at school today?"

"You got *all* your spelling words right?"

"No."

"A-a-a-ah, you got to see a movie?"

"No."

"Well, I guess I have to give up."

With a smile from ear to ear, Jenay preceded to tell what happened: "A boy in my class came up to me and said: 'Guess what I Know! *You're adopted!'* "

As she repeated the boy's "accusation," Jenay jumped up and down, wide-eyed and pointing, in imitation of her classmate's peculiar antics. Then she broke into delighted giggles.

As Jenay's little story illustrates, people look at adoption in very different ways. The meaning of adoption for Jenay was not at all what it was for her classmate. Why is there such a difference? The main reason probably has to do with how we learn what any word means—that is, by the way we hear the word used in our own experience.

Jenay has come to know what adoption means as a member of our family. She knows simply that I am "Dad," that Ebeth is "Mom," that Jon (11 years old) is her big brother, that Geoff (13 years old) is her bigger brother, and that Sasha (three years old) is her little sister.

From the time she was a toddler we have talked about adoption as a natural part of our family conversation. From her earliest memories she has heard that to be adopted is to be part of our family. "There are two ways that we can become part of a family," Ebeth and I have often explained to our children. "One way is by being born out of Mom's stomach." (I admit the description is a little imprecise; the anatomical designations have been made more exact as the children have grown older.) "That's the way Geoff and Jon and Sasha came into our family. The second way is that you can come into a family by being adopted. Jenay came into our family this way because the lady whose stomach she was in wanted her to have a good home and a good family and she couldn't provide them herself."

We realize that this does not answer all the questions. Nor can we always expect to have an uncomplicated answer. Moreover, the meaning of adoption as found in our family will come into conflict with other meanings, as it did in the example above. It is likely that these conflicts will become sharper as our children grow older and are exposed to wider experiences. Though we can imagine some of these conflicts, it does little good to dwell on potential problems. We must simply live day by day, trusting in the sufficiency of God's grace for whatever the future holds.

In our family the meaning of adoption is part of our whole understanding of life as rooted in the Christian faith. Thus, when we explain to our children what adoption means, we often add, "Mom and Dad are adopted too." As Christians, we have been adopted into God's family, we have become God's children (Gal. 4:5).[1] With this understanding adoption takes on the highest possible meaning and significance. I would suggest that we all might profit from reflecting upon this basic Christian truth, with respect to both our relationship to God and our relationship to our parents or children whether adopted or not.

In looking to the Christian idea of being adopted into the family of God, we can see what adoption ideally should be. But more than this, many of these same principles are applicable to any family relationship; for to be adopted into God's family is to be a child of God in the fullest sense. As adopted children (whether as part of God's family or as part of a human family) there is no sense in which this is a "second class" relationship. We are fully children of the family with all the privileges and responsibilities that any child enjoys, whether adopted or not (see Gal. 4:1-7).

Whether we speak of "spiritual" (i.e., adoption into God's family) or human adoption, the adoption process starts with a need. Spiritually we are lost, separated from God, without a home. Likewise, the child who will be adopted is in need of a human home. From the point of view of the adoptive family, the circumstances surrounding this need really are unimportant. God does not ask for our credentials to see whether we are good enough—or for that matter bad enough—to be received into His family. No, God's grace is sufficient and his offer is made to us whatever our circumstances. Likewise if a child is in genuine need of a home, and if God has called us to share in this particular need, His grace will be sufficient.[2] As a result, the emphasis changes from our need and the circumstances of our need to, through God's grace, our potential. Likewise, in a human family, the need of an adopted child is transformed into hope and promise.

Though the adoption process starts with a need, this need can be met only where it is responded to through a decision or choice. As Christians being "spiritually" adopted, the Apostle Paul writes that "God chose us to be His very own"*(Eph. 1:4, LB)*. Likewise a child who is adopted into a human family is chosen to be part of our very own family. But we must recognize that such a choice—whether we speak of God's choice of us or our "choosing" a child in need—this choice is not an arbitrary *fiat*: it is not a single event in past time that has no bearing upon the present and future. Such a choice results in a relationship that is eternal—a relationship in which God's loving care, His sustaining grace, is lavished upon us. Likewise, on the human level, as parents of an adopted child we are called to a continuing relationship of loving care for the child which God in his providence has entrusted to our choice.

In another sense, being adopted suggests having been given a gift. As spiritually adopted children we recognize that our enterance into God's family has been made possible by God's immeasureable gift of His Son, which in turn makes possible the gift of eternal life (both present and future) to all who place their trust in God. As parents we might say that we too share our lives with our children, whether adopted or not; certainly we are called as Christians to do this. But if we leave the idea of gift-giving here we have only recognized a small part of its

meaning; for today the idea seems to have become
rather shallow and confused. Perhaps we should distin-
guish between giving a *present* and truly giving a *gift*. I'm
afraid that most of the giving that we do is simply on one
level of giving *presents* (though sometimes a present can
also become a true gift). Giving "presents" normally involves some idea of necessity, external requirement,
self-interest or obligatory reciprocity. Giving a true gift
goes beyond all this to the point where the gift is given
out of selfless love. Where this happens, all interest in
reciprocity or reward is overcome; the reward of the gift
to the giver is the act of giving itself. In adopting a child
(or in raising any child) it is true that we are giving a gift;
but what we receive in return is far greater than any
measure we might place upon our own giving. Ebeth
and I must give to our family (and God knows we are not
always gracious about it), but the gifts that we receive
from each of our children go far beyond efforts.

The recognition that adoption involves a giving relationship needs to be complemented, however, by an appreciation for the *objective, legal* basis of adoption. It is
interesting to note that the Apostle Paul actually used the
Roman legal understanding of adoption into a human
family to explain the *Christian* meaning of adoption into
God's family (see Gal. 4:1-7). It follows that we should
not try to "de-institutionalize" adoption in our own society into a sentimental, subjective, individualized arrangement. Adoption must have an objective basis in law
and must be carried out in compliance with all the legal
formalities. Failure to do so can result in serious problems if not tragedy.

Using the analogy of Roman law, the Apostle Paul
recognizes "spiritual" adoption as a "legal" fact. The
Christian, by adoption, is "legally" a full-fledged member

of God's family. There is nothing second-rate about this status, nothing to apologize about. As Christians God has adopted us "as his very own sons" (Gal. 4:5, *LB*); we have the Spirit of his Son in our hearts; "we are full heirs to all that is His" (vs.7). Similarly then, we may speak of adoption into a human family in the same terms. Again there is nothing second-rate about this status, nothing to apologize about. There are simply two ways to become part of a family—either on the basis of a biological fact, or on the basis of a legal fact. From a Christian point of view there is no important difference.

Even though a child may be part of a family either by virtue of biology or adoption, neither of these facts are sufficient in themselves. In either case, the family is an unfolding reality—a living, growing relationship. The reality of the objective fact must take shape in the lives of both parents and children in a relationship of trust and love, and of authority and responsibility. Again we can look to God's relationship to his own (adopted!) children for the pattern of how we are to relate to our children. Thus we are to be, like God is, loving and long-suffering, patient and kind, just and righteous; and where necessary we must chastize those for whom we have been given responsibility.

From a Christian point of view then, adoption takes on a special meaning. It begins with a need, which is just as much a promise; it brings us to a choice which is transformed into a sacred trust; it becomes a gift in which the one who gives is really the one who receives; it is established by a legal fact which becomes an unfolding relationship of trust and love. The Christian meaning of adoption holds up an ideal which is rooted in what God has done for us in Christ Jesus. yet each of us as parents can recognize our own failure to realize the ideal as God has intended. In this sense we are still children, we are still far from maturity, and must therefore call upon our (adoptive!) Father in Heaven for forgiveness and guidance and grace to become what he would have us be.

[1]The idea of being adopted into God's family is a prominent feature in the Apostle Paul's description of the Christian life and salvation. St. Paul uses adoption (Greek: *huiothesia*) five times in this connection all refering to our relationship to God as Christians. Though the Greek word clearly refers to adoption, English versions translate *huiothesia* in different ways. Most English translations use "adoption" in Romans 8:23 and Gal. 4:5; but Rom. 8:15 and 9:4 use the English word "sonship" while Eph. 1:5 is translated "to be his sons." The interchangability of "adopted sonship" and "non-adopted sonship" reflects both the Christian and Roman legal understanding that the relationship is identical, as we shall explain further below.

[2]I say "*if* God has called us to share in this particular need" because adoption clearly is not everyone's calling. There are many other needs to which as Christians God may call us to help meet. Adoption is the calling of a relatively few and should not distract us from the need to reach out to the world in many other ways.

PART ONE
THE ADOPTION EXPERIENCE

1 / What Color Is Love?

Dale Evans Rogers

Ever since I was a child, I wanted a large family. My mother's family consisted of seven girls and one boy, and my father's had three boys and four girls. There was a beautiful, special warmth in those family gatherings that I have carried in my heart through the years. When I was about nine years old, I dreamed of marrying Tom Mix and having six children. Little did I realize that one day I would actually be married to a movie cowboy and have, altogether during that marriage, not six but nine children!

When Roy Rogers and I married New Year's Eve, 1947, I had a grown son by my first marriage. Roy had an adopted daughter, one of his own by his late wife, and also a baby son. In 1950 Robin Elizabeth, our little "Angel Unaware," retarded with a defective heart, was born to Roy and me. She blessed our lives for two years and returned to her Heavenly Father.

Two months prior to her death, I visited Hope Cottage in Dallas, Texas, to inquire about the parents of Roy's adopted daughter. She was now in her early teens and I felt the need of advice on questions she was asking. While there, I visited the Cottage nursery. In the middle of the room was a light olive child with enormous, beautiful dark brown eyes, topped by a thick thatch of straight blue-black hair. She was two and a half months old. Raising herself up on little elbows, she watched me intently all around the nursery. This child completely captivated me. I asked about her ancestry and was told, "Choctaw Indian with a bit of Scotch-Irish." Her name was Mary. The attendant said Mary must go to a home where there was Indian blood. I thought, "Roy has Choctaw blood." Then I said to the nurse, "Somebody is going to get a beautiful child!" Little did I know we would be the lucky ones.

In September, three weeks after losing our little Robin and still numbed by it, Roy and I were on our way to New York for the rodeo in Madison Square Garden. We stopped to visit my parents in Italy, Texas, and just before leaving on the plane Roy suggested we visit Hope Cottage. Perhaps it would make me feel better to see some babies. Walking up the steps of the Cottage, I suddenly remembered little Mary and asked if she was still there. The lady in charge said that Mary was ready for adoption and a Dallas woman with Indian blood was coming the next day to see the baby. I asked to see Mary and immediately reached for her. My heart went out to this child and she responded, whereupon I asked Roy if we could adopt her. He loves children and said, "If you want her, I want her." There was a bit of family opposition because it was felt that Roy and I had enough family, but we listened to our own aching hearts. We needed this child and she needed us. The Cottage promised to let us know in a couple weeks.

When we received the call from Dallas saying we

might pick up Mary on our way to Los Angeles, I let out a shout that probably filled Manhattan! Following the Madison Square Garden engagement we were to do some one night engagements on the way home. In Cincinnati at the auditorium we met a little boy from a welfare home in Kentucky. He had been abandoned at eight months old and left to starve in a motel—with severe rickets due to malnutrition. He had no bridge to his nose, poor coordination and a slight astigmatism in one eye. But when that little fellow smiled, all heaven broke loose! We were "had" on the spot. He was five years old. We inquired of his custodian if adoption was possible. She was quite honest about his background, which was not good. We told her we would ponder it, pray about it and give her a call from our hotel room that night.

In our room after the show we did just that. Roy finally said, "Anyone will take a kid that has everything going for him, but what happens to a little guy like that?" He was silent for a moment and then announced, "Let's take him!" I agreed. We called the custodian, who called the welfare worker, who called a judge. It was decided we could take the little boy with us the next day, after signing the necessary papers in Covington, just across the river from Cincinnati. None of the rest of our family knew about this new addition, although we had called them about bringing little Mary home with us. I had already named her Merry "Little Doe," an Indian name.

Once Roy and I had made the decision to take Sandy, we never looked back. We knew he was a neglected, abused child and probably had emotional problems. Though we did not know it at the time, Sandy also had slight brain damage. Our pediatrician said he had either been dropped and hit his head between the eyes, or had been hit with a fist. The doctor was inclined to believe the latter. When we first took him for evaluation and shots, our doctor frankly said, "You people have a lot of courage to take a child in this condition." We told him it was a privilege to help such a child and we intended to do what we could for him. At an examination two years later this same doctor said it was a miracle to see what loving care had done in this space of time.

We sent Sandy to a remedial school for reading in the first grade and he finally was able to read well enough to attend regular classes in public school, though it was nip and tuck for him. Up till then he had been mostly with retarded or afflicted children in the welfare home and had experienced no companionship with completely normal children.

In 1954, while on a theater tour of Great Britain and appearing at Haringay Arena in London with Billy Graham, we met a lovely little 11-year-old girl in a Church of Scotland orphanage in Edinburgh. This child was an orphan of divorce and had been placed, along with a brother and sisters, in orphanages to stay until age 15, at which time she could choose the parent with whom she wished to reside. Her father had custody. Her name was Marion, and she had a personality as fresh as Scottish heather. We obtained permission to have her visit us the following summer. After the visit it was unthinkable to send her back. After much correspondence and telephoning to Edinburgh, we gained permission to be her foster parents until she reached age 21.

One year later, Dr. Bob Pierce of World Vision showed a film in our home that melted our hearts. So many little G.I.-Korean orphans, with a very dim future. We looked at Dodie, now three, and thought how wonderful it would be for her to have a Korean sister the same age. Dr. Pierce took a photograph of Dodie to Korea and matched her with a lovely little Korean-Puerto Rican child named In Ai Lee. In about nine months we met our little Korean daughter, whom we already named "Debbie Lee," at the Los Angeles airport.

My son, Tom, our eldest, was now married with a family of his own and teaching school in Northern California.

I would be less than truthful to say there were no problems in our "international family." But let me say with all my heart that our lives were enriched beyond measure by our chosen children. They brought a new dimension into the lives of all of us, and though there were differences of opinion from time to time, we closed ranks and became a family "one in the spirit and one in the Lord." Once in a while, the subject of adoption would come up and I would simply say, "We are all adopted into the family of God through our Lord Jesus Christ; therefore we all have adoption in common." Then I would explain that earthly parents are simply caretakers for God, whether the children are natural children by birth or chosen by adoption. It is wonderful that adopted children seem to take on characteristics of their adopted families and finally resemble them. Come to think of it, God was very, very gracious to us humans when he instituted the family. . . .

We were a varied lot. The children included a boy born in Tennessee (my son, Tom); a boy and girl of English extraction born in Los Angeles (Roy's daughter and son); a girl of English extraction and one of Indian extraction born in Dallas; a Nordic-type boy from Kentucky; a Scotch-Irish girl from Scotland, and a Korean-Puerto Rican girl from Seoul, Korea. Their dad was

from Ohio, of German-Scottish-Irish-Indian extraction,
and their mom was of English-Scottish-Irish extraction
from Texas.

One day our little Indian maid asked me, "Why do you
stay so white and I get so brown in the summer?" I
replied that God's garden is made up of many flowers of
beautiful, different colors, and would be pretty dull if the
flowers were all the same. So it was with people, for they
are His human garden. Since we were all created, according to the Bible, through Christ, God sees us all as equal
and beautiful, for He simply does not make mistakes. A
very talented friend of mine, Joy Eilers, wrote a haunt-
ingly beautiful song: "What Color Is Love?" That song
really tells it like it is, for the color of God is LOVE.

On a television interview, I was asked: "Don't you
realize that in adopting all these children you are just
asking for it? One has enough trouble raising one's own,
without asking for extra trouble by adoption."

Let's face the facts. All families have problems. To be
very honest, though, there are extra problems with
adopted children. When they reach their teens, especially the girls, questions come that are hard to
answer—questions about why they were released for
adoption and why the adoptive parents wanted them. At
least, I found it so. However, by the Grace of God, I tried
to be as honest as I could with our children. I told them
we adopted them because we loved them and wanted
them when we saw them—and we wanted them to be a
part of us.

Some people said, "What if these children go looking
for their own parents when they are older, and perhaps
reject you? How will you feel then?" I responded that
God had allowed me the privilege of rearing them and I
would always have my memories of the wonderful ex-

periences we had shared. No one could take this from me. I still feel that way, now that they are all gone from our home. Two of them have gone to their Heavenly Home, Debbie in a church bus accident, and Sandy in a foolish dare in the Armed Forces in Germany.

If I had it to do all over again, I would adopt these children. We chose them because we wanted to share what we were and had with children who had nothing to give us in return but themselves. I feel it was a good deal both ways. As adoptive parents we certainly made mistakes, but we tried our best. I believe the lives of our natural children were greatly enriched by sharing with our chosen ones. We have loved and appreciated them all, and they have blessed us more than they will ever know. Simply bearing a child does not necessarily make one a good mother any more than planting the seed makes one a good father. It's the day-to-day loving, caring and discipline—and sharing a common faith in Almighty God as Heavenly Father through His Son, Jesus Christ—that really counts.

I just wish I could fill this big house all over again with the sounds of children. The years have passed too quickly and the house is so quiet—too quiet.

Thank You, Lord, for allowing me to have a husband who let me be "Mom" to chosen children as well as our own natural ones.

2 / Heaven's Special Children

Bonnie Wheeler

My husband and I sat nervously waiting for the social worker to finish reviewing our application for an adopted child. What would be her reaction to the many trials and troubles we'd had with our natural children? Julie, born with cerebral palsy. Timmy, hyperactive as a result of a head injury. Robby, needing five operations before reaching his second year.

Finally, she looked at us and asked, "Mr. and Mrs. Wheeler, how can you possibly want to adopt a child? Especially, as I see on your application, a handicapped one?"

We shared with the puzzled social worker our faith and daily walk with Jesus Christ. We also shared our firm belief that God never gives us more than we can handle.

One of the added blessings of the Christian walk is the ability God gives us to seek lessons when we go through trials. We can learn. Not just cry out, "Why me?" as the world does. (Believe me, though, there were days when I did my share of crying.)

God took me in His arms and loved me; He gave me peace, comfort and strength. After the tears were dried, there came a time of asking ourselves and the Lord, "What can we learn from our painful experiences?"

We still wanted another child and were experienced in the problems of "special" children. As we told the social worker, "Every parent would prefer normal children (if there is such a thing!). But if there's a handicapped child without a family, that's the one we want."

We were keenly aware of all that Julie had gone through while being loved and secure. What must it be like for a child trying to cope with similar problems without that loving security?

With this motivation and much prayer, our family embarked on an adventure-filled journey that turned our braces into blessings and our tears into triumph.

In those early days, we gathered around the table for many conferences with the children. We decided on a girl to balance our family—or so we thought at the time. We preferred a child with cerebral palsy because of our familiarity with it. We wanted her younger than Robby. The race was important. Timmy (the only blond) is *our* family minority. He wanted "a pretty little black girl, with an Afro the color of my hair." Some orders are hard to fill!

We discussed problems the children might encounter if we adopted a black child. I was raised in the South and prepared them for the worst (it hasn't happened yet). We asked them what they would do if someone called them, or their new sister, derogatory names. Timmy and Robby's charitable, Christian answer? "Punch their lights out!"

At last! We heard about a little girl: Black-Oriental; three years old; cerebral palsy. She was just what we had "ordered."

I'll never forget our first visit with Becky—I was scared half to death! And I certainly was surprised that being checked out and approved by a three-year-old could be so nerve-racking.

Becky couldn't walk, and her sitting balance was so poor that she was constantly tipping over. I was generally afraid she'd break. In comparing first impressions, Dennis was not as afraid as I was. He just saw a little girl that needed him.

"Are you going to be my new mommy and daddy?" was the first question she asked us. After our affirmative answer, she started referring to her foster parents as "Old Mommy" and "Old Daddy" (I'm sure they loved that).

The foster parents and social worker prepared us for a lengthy adjustment period because of Becky's inability to handle changes. Just the month before, the foster family had gone camping. Becky became so hysterical when they changed camping sites that she required sedation.

"If that upset her so much, what will happen when she changes families, names and cities?" With this question in mind, we planned on two months of visits to make it less traumatic for Becky.

After her first overnight visit, Becky wanted to stay with us! The move was made almost six weeks sooner than we *adults* had planned. No one but me was able to comprehend Becky's positive reaction. Since we first started adoption proceedings, I had prayed on a daily basis, "Lord, I know You already have a child selected. Prepare her heart for us." Boy, did He ever!

The foster mother and social worker were honest and open with us. We were warned that Becky became genuinely hysterical over many things—slamming doors, being by herself, any change. Some days she'd just bawl all day for no apparent reason. Dennis and I made an advance agreement: when Becky had that crying spell I could leave when he came home from work. It's been almost three years and I haven't made that hasty exit yet.

Dennis and I have both felt the Lord's leading so strongly that we were afraid not to adopt. "The greatest calamity is not to have failed, but to have failed to try."

Well-meaning friends and relatives were constantly telling us how brave or how stupid we were. If I had a trying day with Becky, their words would haunt me. The Lord always reassured us, though, that we were in His will and this was *the* child He wanted us to have. My daily prayer became, "Lord, help me remember that nothing will happen today that You and I can't handle *together.*"

Becky was going through a difficult period herself. After one particularly rough day, she rapidly folded her hands for bedtime prayers and said, "Dear Lord, please don't believe a thing my mother tells you."

One of our conflicts was over Becky's eating habits. She usually likes breakfast and lunch, but dinner she could do without. There was one breakfast, though, that she didn't like at all. I had done my "super mommy" routine and fixed hit cereal. She took one bite, gagged, spit it out and glared at me saying, "My foster mother never made me eat *this!*"

Dinners were worse. If I fixed one of her two favorite menus she would eat. But if she'd never seen or heard of a particular food I served—not a bite!

I later learned that this is a common problem with non-ambulatory children. First, they're not burning up as many calories as walking, running, jumping children. Secondly, they have so little control over their life that they enjoy (at least) having control over what they eat.

There were days when we could have used a degree in psychiatry. Becky hadn't been taught to do anything for herself and was completely dependent on others.

Becky was very fearful of slamming doors. With a windy city and three committed door-slammers, this really got to be a problem. I tried talking to the other children. Just about the time they really made an effort to be careful, a big gust of wind would come through and *bang!* another case of hysterics.

One day I decided to show Becky how to slam a door. She slammed it and screamed. I had her slam it again. She screamed (but not quite as loud). By the third slam, she thought it was great fun. Then I showed her how to open the door, and we had one problem licked.

Often when Becky awoke, she would scream. The first week I thought (by the noise) that King Kong had broken into her room; my heart would start pounding; I'd run into her room; breathlessly, I'd ask, "What's wrong?" Calmly, she'd reply, "I want up." One day I wasn't feeling well. The scream came; I ran in; she wanted up. "Then get up yourself," I told her. Becky stared at me, saw I was serious, tried and did it. At three, she had gotten out of bed all by herself. A celebration hug ended both our bad moods. Another problem solved.

Becky arrived potty trained, but I had to pick her up, pull down her panties, set her on the potty chair, then reverse the whole procedure. I soon tired of this, bought the sturdiest chair made and installed it in the bathroom.

Soon after, I heard her call out, "I have to go potty!" "Well, there it is; help yourself." She looked absolutely panic-stricken, but—she did it!

Time after time, I've been confronted by a seemingly unsolvable problem. I'll pray for guidance and *divine* wisdom, but usually the Lord shows me how to apply *common* sense. Our children are not called handicapped and are not treated as if they were. They may move a little slower and not as well, but that's all.

Julie has always wanted a sister and was especially attached to Becky. Becky started using this. If Julie didn't play with her or share a toy, Becky would cry "I'll go back to my foster parents." Then Julie would cry. We tried explaining to Julie that Becky couldn't go back, but it still continued.

One day, Becky wanted a cookie. I told her no. "If you don't give me one, I'll go back to my foster mother," she threatened. "We love you and want you to live with us," I told her. "But, if that's how you really feel, here's a bag. You pack and I'll call your social worker." (This is not recommended procedure.) I dialed T-I-M-E and held the phone. Becky held the paper sack, popped her thumb into her mouth (a sure sign she was thinking) and said, "I'd rather stay here." That ended the threatening game. Later that day, it finally hit me—what would I have done if she had packed?

For parents of adopted children one of the most comforting phrases in the Bible is "and it came to pass." Hearing other adoptive parents share their adjustment problems and how they smoothed out and "came to pass" was invaluable to us.

The first Spring, after Becky joined our family, we had a Japanese exchange student stay with us. One weekend we took our four children (three white, one black), our Japanese student, our very tall Youth Pastor and his wife, and their exchange student and we all went to Carmel-Monterey. We felt like a United Nations parade, and some people evidently thought we were. One lady actually pulled her husband back, to help her sort out our group. To top off our day we went into a *Persian* restaurant for lunch and almost created an international incident. I often think God must have a delightful sense of humor.

"What happens when Becky is old enough to date?" has been our most frequently asked question. In our family will she get to meet enough black fellows? Will the white ones date her? Our answer to that? "If that's our main worry when Becky's fifteen, 'Praise the Lord!' "

We still felt our family incomplete and asked our worker to look for another child. We also felt Becky's adjustment would be easier if she wasn't the only adopted Wheeler. Thus, Benji entered our lives.

Benji was fifteen months old, black-Mexican. His medical dossier was hardly encouraging: possibly retarded (he slept most of his first ten months); cerebral palsy (our specialty); respiratory and digestive problems. Then we saw his picture. All our intelligent well-planned notions flew out the window—it was love at first sight!

We went to visit Benji, and when I put out my arms he came right to me. "That's the first time he's ever gone to a stranger," remarked the very surprised foster mother. I had to bite my tongue to keep back the words, "I'm no stranger—I'm his mother."

At fifteen months, Benji wheezed like a train, could only eat very strained baby foods, had just started to sit up and didn't walk or crawl. He also didn't respond to people, look at himself in a mirror and was considered at least six months behind.

The day Benji arrived he was wearing his *entire* wardrobe! I had prayed, "Lord, do I have a prayer request for You." He heard and He really answered! That first week we received phone calls from three different families: "We've been saving clothes and hear you have a new toddler."

All those clothes were the right size! From worrying about how we could afford to outfit Benji, he's become the best dressed member of the family.

During the weeks of waiting, and after Benji's arrival, we were constantly beseeching God for His guidance. Time and again during my daily devotions the Lord gave us reassurances that we were in His will. Our favorite verse became Matthew 18:5: "And whosoever shall receive one such little child in my name receiveth me." This verse was in my Bible reading, daily devotional book, at Benji's dedication and in cards from friends.

The week we became Benji's parents we also became youth sponsors for the junior high group. We felt it was too soon to put Benji in the nursery, so we took him with us. The teens went wild over him, and he was passed around like a football.

The next week I took Benji in to see our pediatrician. I was told, "When some children are in an insecure environment, some withdraw like Benji. He needs an overdose of people. Take him around as many people as possible and let them *pass him around like a football.*" I burst out laughing, "You see, we have these junior highers. . . ." Once again, we saw the Lord answering a prayer before we prayed it, giving a solution before we knew the need.

I'm often asked, "Can you ever feel the same about an adopted child as a homemade one?" We feel that all of our children are loaned to us by God. We have no extra claims on any one. Let me assure you that those first moments when I held Benji and said "I love you" were every bit as exciting and precious as similar movements in the hospital with our newborns.

There were a few adjustment problems between Becky and Benji. The first discovery Benji made was that Becky tipped over easily. Since she was often on the floor, Benji assumed she wanted to play. He was constantly pushing her over. He's laugh with glee at his great new game. Becky just screamed.

Our first month with Benji was one of constant excitement. He gained almost three pounds, grew two inches and started walking and talking. By the time he was eighteen months old, we had him tested at Child Development Center. He was *on* age level (that's almost a year's development in three months); the retarded label was officially removed; and hardly any signs of the cerebral palsy remained.

When I shared the good news with our pediatrician, he picked Benji up, held him close and said, "You're one of the lucky ones, Ben. Half the world just needs lovin' and the other half is usually afraid to give it."

Becky was steadily making progress, but hers was slower than Benji's. Every time Benji said a new word or did something new we felt like we'd been handed a treasure. I even began to pity people who just expected these signs of development and took them for granted.

What lessons we have learned about speech, sturdy legs and bright minds. What treasures they are! Our family also gained a unique sense of accomplishment during this time: *if we supplied the love, God supplied the miracles!*

We always knew that when Becky turned five she would have extensive surgery on both feet and legs. As the time grew nearer, I grew more and more apprehensive. I was afraid that the pain and discomfort of the surgery and five months in casts would undo all our progress.

I started preparing Becky for the hospital: "Becky, you know this will hurt some. . . ." But before I could finish, I was interrupted. . . . "Don't worry Mommy. If it hurts, they'll just give me a shot. My friend told me all about it."

Kids are so resilient—the only negative memory Becky's friend had was the bad food.

This year, another friend of Becky's went in for surgery. Becky got to pass on advice: "It's just awful; they take away your panties and your *buns* get cold." Four hours of surgery, five months in casts and all she remembered was "cold buns."

Becky's surgery was supposed to prevent further problems, not really help her walking. Somewhere along the line, Becky either didn't hear that or decided to ignore it.

Four months after the casts were removed, she walked across the family room—no crutches, no braces, and no holding on. Her sitting balance is also about 95 percent improved. Her surgeon attributes it to luck; we call it answered prayer!

Our lives have been enriched in so many other ways. Our church has truly become our church *family*. We have "adopted" grandparents from the congregation. They share holidays with us, have the children over night and really fill a void in our lives. Other church friends serve as aunts and uncles.

We have started several Wheeler traditions aimed at developing the children's sense of self worth. Each of us has a night to say grace. Benji learned "Juliday" and "Timmyday" before he ever heard of Monday and Tuesday.

We also feature a different child at dinner or devotions. The featured child gets to choose the menu or devotions, and the others do his evening chores. We each tell something special we like about them and we pray for them. Some evenings we sing our version of a favorite song: ". . . red and yellow, black and white. They're at Wheeler's house tonight."

Becky is now six. In September, she starts first grade at our neighborhood school. We're slightly apprehensive about her leaving the protected environment of her special school, but we know it's a necessary step.

Benji is three and loves nursery school. His only problem is a slight slowness in speech.

Encouraged by the miraculous progress Becky and Benji were making, we started the process for a sixth child. We wanted another girl to balance out the family (seems I've heard that before). We specified between the ages of four and ten, and once again, didn't specify the race or handicap. Jokingly, I told our social worker, "After the very vocal Becky I wouldn't mind a mute."

During this time dear friends were trying to get custody of a little girl who was legally blind, deaf and mute. I spent many hours talking with my friend to see if she was looking at the situation realistically and could handle the child. I entered the little girl's name (Alicia) in my prayer diary, little realizing how the Lord would answer my prayer. A problem arose and our friends didn't get Alicia.

Several months later we received a call from our social worker: "We have a girl you might be interested in. She's almost nine, her mother had rubella and she's legally deaf, blind and mute."

"What a funny coincidence," we thought. "How many children like that can there be in the Bay area?" *Her name was Alicia.* Alicia's social worker had heard of us through AASK (Aid to Adoption of Special Kids). Everywhere we turned there was this child. At this point we had to stop and ask: "Do meaningless coincidences happen in the lives of Christians?"

"Lord, you wouldn't ask this of us, would you?" Leg braces, wheelchairs and therapy don't phase us. We are

used to them and know how to cope with them. But here
was a whole new frightening vocabulary: deaf, blind,
mute, sign language and hearing aids. We were both
really scared.

There was much prayer, searching through the Scriptures and a growing belief that Alicia kept coming up for
a purpose. With all these apprehensions we went to visit
Alicia for the first time.

The social worker had arranged for us to observe
Alicia at her school. I had prayed that the Lord would
give us that spark of identity we had with Becky and
Benji—that spark that says, "This is our child and we can
cope." I especially prayed that the Lord would work
through Dennis.

Alicia checked out the parade of strangers that day
and decided she wanted Dennis. The social workers and
I spent that first visit watching Dennis and his *new daughter* getting acquainted.

We went out to lunch afterwards to sort out our first
impressions. They were more favorable than we'd expected. Alicia is tiny (only 36 lbs.), she has some hearing,
and peripheral vision in one eye. Dennis saw a little girl
that was going to need a lot of work and a lot of love. In
typical female fashion, I wanted to feed her, fix her hair
and dress her up.

As we started telling people about Alicia, we received a
funny reaction. When we told friends about Becky and
Benji everyone had asked, "Are you sure you can handle
this?" Now when we really weren't sure at all, everyone
was saying, "What's to be scared of? Look at Becky and
Benji."

We had to be careful at this point. Everyone was talking about miracles and surgeries and vast improvements
in Alicia (and we still pray for all of them to happen). But

we had to be realistic. What if she didn't change? Didn't improve? Our key words at this point became: *expect a miracle but don't demand it.*

When we told our worker that we wanted Alicia (she wasn't surprised) we were told it would take *at least* six months. Another complete home study had to be made and *then* the placement. The more we saw of Alicia the more upset we became. The foster home she was in was like a mini-institution. There were five other children, all deaf-blind and retarded. Since the deaf-blind learn by imitation everyone concerned felt that Alicia needed the stimulation and example of "normal" kids. It struck me as very ironic that after all my efforts at getting Becky and Benji's labels removed here was officialdom calling our children "normal."

Our big concern was that Alicia was at a crucial age. Six months might mean the difference between a successful future for her—or a wasted one. I was growing more and more frustrated at the thought of her being "lost." We asked several friends to pray for the Lord's timing in all of this.

We were supposed to go away on vacation and at the last minute decided to stay home and take day trips in our area. The first day of our vacation, I called our social worker and said (as Dennis prayed), "We're growing more concerned about Alicia and think the sooner she can join our family the better. Can anything be done?" She wasn't too enthusiastic but said she'd check. As I hung up I turned it over to the Lord.

Two days later, Alicia's worker called saying, "We're going to court Friday and get an order, placing Alicia in your home—*immediately!*" No waiting, no licensing or home study first. Talk about answered prayer!

If we'd gone out of state for our vacation, we'd have

missed the phone calls and both workers would have been gone on their vacations when we returned. God's perfect timing.

As I write this, we've had Alicia a month. It's been a very tiring yet exciting month. All of us are learning sign language so we can better communicate with her. Right now it's like learning to swim when you're thrown in the water.

We've had some fun experiences with the sign language. One day I had a completely silent argument with Alicia. She got fed up with me and got sassy and signed a steady stream of "no" at me. Getting yelled at, she'll turn off her hearing aids.

Robby first learned the sign for "hug." Every time he saw Alicia he'd ask for one. Now no matter what he signs she just sighs deeply and gives him a hug.

Alicia can't understand this strange custom of ours where we say grace. But she's learning. One day she wanted seconds, and instead of signing "more" she folded her hands, as in prayer, and waited.

The tiring part is obvious to anyone who's read about Helen Keller. Without words there is no way to express love, rage, fears and frustrations. The job now is to get all those words (in sign) into Alicia.

I pray daily for strength. The rubella kids don't sleep well. Neither do their parents. We spend the day with Alicia wanting to take her shoes off and not playing with her toys. We spend the nights with Alicia wanting to put her shoes on and play with her toys. When I have a rough time and wonder if I can handle this, the Lord reminds me, once again, that we are in this together.

People often ask if we don't expect too much of our children, especially the older ones. We talk about this sort of thing often. The kids' answer? "We're a family. And families work together."

Julie does most of our babysitting (and she's first asked, then paid). She's more capable and unafraid than most adults. Because of their close ages, Robby and Becky are often together at school and church. He pushes her wheelchair frequently giving her added mobility. He also gets into arguments with people who doubt that they're brother and sister.

Dennis and I recently had a severe case of the flu and Julie was gone. Eleven-year-old Timmy volunteered and took over for the day—feeding kids, washing dishes and getting aspirin and juice for us. Each child watches out for Alicia. These days she's into and exploring everything, and no one human can keep up with her. Yes, our children have more responsibilities than their peers but the rewards far outweigh the responsibilities—they get to live on an everyday basis with miracles.

This year Becky was "mainstreamed" into a regular first grade class at our neighborhood school. Benji is on age level and in love with his nursery school teacher.

Will Alicia have her miracle, like Becky and Benji? Will she make vast improvements? Or stay the same?

I don't yet know what Alicia's future holds but I do know that all I *have seen* helps me to trust all that I have *not* seen.

This poem by an unknown author was on a plaque Becky gave us one Christmas.

Heaven's Very Special Child

A meeting was held quite far from earth
"It's time again for another birth."
The angels said to the Lord above,
"This dear little child will need much love.

His progress on earth may be quite slow
Accomplishments great he may not show .
And he will require some extra care
From the folks he meets on earth down there.
He may never run or laugh or play;
His thoughts may seem odd and far away.
In various ways he won't adapt,
And he will be known as handicapped.
Please, Lord, find some parents for this child
Who'll do this good work as unto you.
They'll not understand it right away—
The difficult role You'd have them play;
But with this dear child sent from above
Comes strength, and new faith and richer love.
And soon they will know the priv'lege giv'n
To care for this gift that's straight from Heaven.
This precious child, so meek and mild
Will always remain *Thy special child!*"

3 / "Can You Take This Child?"

Diny Bailey

Romans 8:28—"And we know that all things work together for good to them that love God, to them who are the called according to his purpose."

How true this has been for me. God certainly was working in my life even before I really knew Him! After having led a very sheltered life in the small town of Oisterwijk in the Netherlands, I immigrated to America at the age of 18 and moved in with some distant relatives. Sometime later I married and gave birth to a girl, Maryann, and then two years later to a boy, Teddy.

Due to circumstances I found myself returning to work and leaving my children with a baby sitter. I had thought that she was giving my children good care. Then one day I returned home early from work and found both children locked outside the house in the blazing sun. The baby sitter was inside taking a nap. Teddy was still in diapers, and I could tell that he hadn't been changed in quite a while. Maryann, a bright three year old, had wet her pants because the baby sitter wouldn't allow her in the house to use the toilet. At this point I came to the decision that I would quit my job and baby-sit in my home for the children of other working parents.

I really enjoyed working with the little children. I found out, though, that some of these kids came from homes where foul language was just about all they heard. During the week I worked with them to clean up their vocabulary to the point where they wouldn't swear any-more. However, after they returned from a weekend at home, we would have to start the process again. As this was very frustrating and discouraging, I decided to do boarding care.

The first child we got was a newborn baby from an unwed mother. One day after three months the natural mother walked in, took the baby and left. Again, disap-pointment and frustration. I was licensed by the Illinois Department of Children and Family Services (IDCFS), and I called them to voice my discouragement. They in turn asked if I had ever considered foster care. I replied that I would first have to discuss it with my husband. The following day I again called the IDCFS and told them my husband and I would be willing.

It turned out they had been looking for a foster home for a six-month-old orphaned baby girl. She had been placed in an institution at birth because of severe physical deformities. These handicaps had led the doctors to be-lieve that she was brain damaged too. However, this as-sumption proved false, for after a few months in the institution she was responding normally. The authorities now began looking for the right kind of home for this "special" baby.

On that first visit to meet Beth, I realized that she wouldn't look like my daughter did as a baby. But I expected her to be dressed attractively and held in the arms of a caring nurse. My heart dropped when we entered the institution and were led to where Beth lay clad only in a diaper and soiled T-shirt. She was so precious as she laid there helplessly, stretching out her little arms to me to be picked up. I reached down, picked her up, and fell in love with her.

After I returned home I discussed it first with my husband and then together with Maryann, now four, and Teddy. All of us were eager for this new addition to our family.

Beth was born with a severe cleft palate and no roof in her mouth. She had only two or three fingers on each hand, two toes on each foot, no saliva glands and no tear ducts—we never could tell if Beth was laughing or crying when she was a baby.

Because of Beth's handicaps it was necessary to spend many long hours in various clinics. Since Beth had so many different deformities, sometimes she had to be seen by half a dozen different doctors. That meant an entire day spent in the waiting rooms with two restless young children while Beth was being examined.

Despite the open stares from adults and thoughtless remarks by children, we did many things together as a family, including grocery shopping. One day while standing at the checkout counter I noticed that Beth's shoe was untied. We had just taught her how to tie her shoes, and of course it was a struggle for her to do it with only a few fingers on each hand, but she could. So I told Beth to tie her shoe. Evidently, two women in the next aisle heard my remark. Thinking this was awful of me, one of them said, quite loudly, "What a terrible thing to make that helpless youngster do." Everyone else standing in line heard too and began gaping. I didn't reply to those women because obviously they didn't realize that the best thing we could do for Beth was not to shelter her and to instill in her the importance of independence. If Beth didn't learn independence at an early age she would not only become a helpless youngster, but a helpless teen-ager, and worse yet, a helpless misfit of an adult unable to do anything for herself.

Looking back I see the Lord working. The first year Beth was in our home taught me patience, patience learned by waiting long tiring hours in a crowded clinic, and patience learned also by holding my tongue when thoughtless remarks were made to and about Beth.

When Beth was a year and a half our family had another addition. Gordon was two years old when we got him. His natural mother didn't receive any prenatal care, and because of this Gordon was born mentally handicapped. If his mother had had the proper prenatal care it would have been apparent that Gordon's Rh factor was negative and that he would need a blood transfusion immediately after birth. His Rh factor, however, was not determined until 24 hours after his birth—too late. During these first two important years of his childhood he was almost totally neglected. When he came to us he was suffering from malnutrition and was severely emotionally disturbed. In fact, he was so emotionally disturbed that he was on the waiting list to be committed to a mental institution—and he was only two years old!

Gordon joined our family on a trial basis. He couldn't do anything a normal two year old could do. He couldn't talk, walk or feed himself. His hair was almost to the middle of his back, his finger nails were long, and he had literally chewed his tiny hand raw. When we attempted to feed him he wouldn't allow anyone to come near. To try and get him to eat we would put the food in a bowl and place it on the tray of his highchair. Even then he wouldn't eat. It was only after we were out of his sight that he would take his hand from his mouth and eat his food with his hands.

That first evening we put Gordon in his crib he grabbed hold of the bars and began shaking it so hard we thought he would shatter it in half. He stopped only after he had dropped off to sleep in sheer exhaustion. At this point my husband and I experienced doubts. We didn't know if we would be capable of properly handling a child like Gordon. Gradually Gordon improved, however. He began to trust us and he slowly progressed. Six months later he was able to walk, talk and play, and he no longer chewed on his hand. His status was then changed from a trial to a permanent basis. Gordon is 18 now, and even though he is educably mentally handicapped he is a fine young man. He was in our home until he was 16 and then placed in the J. P. Kennedy Foundation School. He needed more care at 16 than we were able to give him.

Donald, a severely retarded youth of 12, joined the family for a while. Again without my knowledge the Lord was teaching me patience. He did quite well but had to leave after two years because of the impact he had on Beth, Gordon and Teddy. He was approaching puberty and was teaching the children some things that weren't right. We called a conference. When this type of situation arises you must always take the family as a whole into consideration. It was best for the family that he left.

While Donald was a part of our family, he did help save Gordon's life. One Saturday morning when we had finished breakfast at nine, Gordon and Donald were playing outside by the swing set. Donald came in and said, "Gordon won't talk to me." Normally we would not have paid any attention to that sort of statement, but fortunately this time we were alarmed. Looking out the back porch window we saw Gordon dangling from a drapery cord by the swing set. We ran out there. My husband gave him mouth to mouth resuscitation and screamed for me to get a knife to cut him loose. Gordon had turned blue. His head looked about twice its normal size, and his tongue was hanging out of his mouth. We cut him loose, and my husband continued with chest pressure and mouth to mouth resuscitation. All of a sudden Gordon let out a yell. Believe me, that was the best yell I've ever heard. Needless to say, after that freaky accident I've never let the children get hold of any rope or drapery cord!

Marlene joined us next. Though 10 years old she had just flunked second grade and was severely emotionally disturbed. Her disturbance was so serious that she was supposed to be only a temporary placement until they could put her in an Ohio institution for severely disturbed children. While we had her with us, we were determined to try and help her. My husband tutored her in school work, and with a lot of counseling on his part and a lot of understanding from the rest of the family, Marlene improved enough so that we were able to keep her. In September on our recommendation she was placed in the fourth grade on a trial basis. After three months she was moved up to fifth grade.

Marlene graduated from high school when she was 18. After that she held a job as a telephone operator for two years, met and married a fine Christian young man and now has two children of her own.

When Maryann was nine, Marlene ten, Teddy seven, Gordon seven and Beth five we were asked if we would like to have another addition to our family. She was a six-week premature baby girl born with a cleft palate.

When I visited her in the hospital she was so tiny—only six pounds at six weeks old. The nurses and doctors said she wasn't gaining fast enough because it tired her out to suck on the bottle. They felt that if I would feed her every hour she might do better. Needless to say we fell in love with her. We were even given the privilege of naming her. Judy joined our family in October and progressed beautifully. At two she had corrective surgery for her cleft palate.

Those who have never adopted children themselves sometimes find it hard to believe adoptive parents when they say they love their children as much as if they were their own "natural" children. But that has been proved over and over again in our family. Judy has brought us continual joy in our lives, and we thank God for sending her to us. She is 11 now and a fine Christian girl. She plays piano and loves to read.

Right after Judy joined us seven-year-old Tony came. Due to family circumstances his sister asked if we would look after him awhile. He was a very smart youngster, and somehow that little while lasted until the present. Tony is 18 years old and graduating from high school as an honor roll student.

Shortly after Tony joined us Angelo came to our family straight from court. He was a six-year-old Puerto Rican boy. When his stepmother dropped him off with the caseworker, big tears rolled down his cheeks. Then he spotted our baby Judy. He took to her right away, and this made him feel more at home. We found out later that he had a baby brother at home. It is really wonderful how the Lord works.

Angelo was a severe uncontrolled diabetic. Sometimes he had to receive as many as four shots of insulin a day. It was really a learning experience with him. Both my husband and I had to learn how to give injections of insulin to Angelo as well as control his diet—all his food had to be measured to the gram! In those days we didn't have disposable syringes so each time we gave Angelo a shot they had to be sterilized. This was quite a chore.

By this time our family was large. Seven children around our dinner table made a noisy meal. It seemed all the children wanted to share their experiences at once. To make sure that no one got slighted, that mom and dad could hear and that everyone got a chance, we had to make a rule. No one could talk at the dinner table unless he raised his hand and mom or dad gave permission. This solved the problem until the kids got older and learned to wait their turn courteously.

It was at this time also that our city was caught in a severe blizzard. It was so terrible that trucks couldn't even get through to the stores with food. Supermarkets began limiting customers to only one loaf of bread and one gallon of milk. With nine hungry mouths to feed, we found it necessary to send each one of the kids separately to the grocery store to purchase his allotment of bread and milk. This made quite a scene as we sent each child to the store with a sled to carry the milk and bread. As soon as one child came back we would send the next one on the way. The kids enjoyed the excitement, and we were able to endure the seven-day siege of snow.

The summer after Angelo came we decided to take a trip to California. Every one of the kids except the baby Judy came along. We had a station wagon at the time, and we purchased a trailer to accommodate us on the trip. This was quite an experience with eight people and a trailer that slept only six. We managed, though, even taking into consideration Angelo's special diet and shot regimen. We didn't have enough money for Disneyland, so as an alternative we went to Knott's Berry Farm. Everyone had a great time. That summer all four boys were eight years old. In order for everyone to have a place to sleep, the boys had to lie widthwise on a double bed in the travel trailer. But they loved it and had a great time telling stories late at night.

We decided to start out on our trip home at 2 A.M. We wanted to cross the desert during the early morning and avoid the unbearable midday heat because we didn't have air-conditioning. There was only one problem. All we had to eat was milk, a few eggs and some peanut butter. The kids were all hungry and there weren't any stores open. But my innovative husband had an idea. He put the raw eggs in the milk, mixed them together thoroughly, and each one of the kids had a full glass of "egg nog"! For protein they each also had a couple tablespoons of peanut butter—not very tasty perhaps but it satisfied them until we could stop at a store.

We were pressed for time the entire vacation because my husband had only two weeks. One day when we were under extreme pressure to reach a certain destination by nightfall Gordon chose to get carsick. We just didn't have the time to stop so we simply rolled down the back window. . . . With all the hardships we had during the trip I felt like a gypsy. But this was the best vacation by far all of us have ever had.

At this time we lived in a big, very comfortable old-fashioned house in the middle of the city. But by the time Marlene was in eighth grade and Maryann in sixth grade the neighborhood began changing. We decided we should start looking for a home in the suburbs. Every Sunday we piled the kids in the car and went looking, but it was very discouraging. The prices were so high and the houses so small. Finally we decided to buy a small home that had been on the market for a long time, but the day that we were going to buy it someone else did. Looking back I realize that this was the Lord working in our life because that house would have been far too small for our needs.

A few weeks later our home in the city sold and we were almost desperate to find another one. That Sunday we decided we would make a decision—if we didn't find a home that day we would just have to buy one in a new sub-division going up. It was that very day that we found the home we are living in today. It was beautiful, big and old-fashioned. It had just come on the market, and the price was within reach. The Lord had it all picked out.

We wanted to do things right when we moved out to the suburbs. Since we were under the impression that everyone here went to church, we went too. While we lived in the city we just sent our kids and never went ourselves except on Easter and Christmas. I remember coming home from church one Easter Sunday and the kids down the street wanting to know where we'd been. Maryann screamed across the street, "You know my parents go to church once a year. Well, today is the day!" We were so embarrassed. It seemed more important than ever that we find a church to attend.

We remembered how Cousin Bart had visited us in the city and had talked about God. We also remembered him saying he went to a Baptist Church. My husband was an atheist, and I was born and raised in the Catholic Church. But Cousin Bart left such a good impression on us that we decided to try the same type of church. I remembered too that even though we had so many children he and his wife had our entire family over for a dinner. This was a real treat for us. With a family our size we seldom got asked over for dinner.

So with all these things in mind we attended a small Baptist Church, and my husband really liked it. In fact, my husband liked that first Sunday so well he wanted to go back for the evening service. This amazed me since he was such a strong atheist. One of the women in the church invited me to come to a Christian Women's Club luncheon. I had a great time. Everybody was so friendly, and I was lonely moving from the city. I had left all my friends behind. When a sheet was passed around for a Bible study, I signed up. I wasn't especially interested in the Bible but I wanted to meet new people. But it was through this Bible study that I began to learn about the Scriptures.

One sweet lady took an interest in me and asked me if I was saved. I said I didn't know. Up to this point I had thought I was a Christian. After all, I was baptized and doing a lot of good things. People were always telling me what marvelous things I was doing by taking in all those children. I would be sure to get a good place in heaven.

In the meantime we kept on faithfully going to church. After three months my husband said he wanted to know more about Christianity and thought we should go to Sunday school too. Therefore, for the first time our family as a unit went to Sunday school and church Our pastor gave an invitation at the end of each sermon, but I never thought it was for me. I figured that by being a good person I was on my way to heaven and didn't need to be saved from hell.

Six months after we moved to the suburbs one of the ladies at the Bible study gave me a tract. I read the message and realized I was a lost sinner, and I took Jesus at his word: "Behold, I stand at the door, and knock; if any man open the door, I will come in and sup with him, and he with me" (Rev. 3:20). It was then that I knelt down in my bedroom and asked Jesus to forgive my sins and come into my heart. That evening there was a special missionary meeting at the church. When they gave the invitation I went forward as a public testimony. I did this because I remembered what Romans 10:9 says: "That if thou shalt confess with thy mouth the Lord Jesus and shalt believe in thine heart that God hath raised him from the dead, thou shalt be saved."

The following Sunday my husband, the atheist, who had an answer for everything when it came to religion, went forward when the invitation was given. After he became a Christian he was a changed man. The first thing he did was pour all the liquor in the house down the drain and burn the "not so nice" books in the fireplace. After this the children also came to know the Lord one by one. Our life took on a new meaning. We were now in the service of the King raising homeless children which He had given us. As the children grew older and started asking questions we gave them answers from the Bible. Moses was a foster child, and the Lord used him mightily. Even the Lord Jesus had a foster father. We taught the children that God put them in our family for a reason and that it was God's will that they were here.

All the children, even the little ones, have chores to do. There are milk bottles to carry out or dirty clothes to bring down to the washing machine. No two children get the same punishment. When they were little, we had lots of corners in the house. When they got bigger we would give them an extra night of dishwashing, or take away TV privileges a couple of nights or make them stay in their room. We had to find out what hurt the most with each individual child and that was the punishment. We used it and stuck with it. "Chasten thy son while there is hope, and let not thy soul spare for his crying" (Prov. 19:18).

When Judy started school I began praying that the Lord might give us another baby to raise. I love little kids. In the meantime I started baby-sitting again, and the Lord used me to witness for Him in this area. My prayer for another baby seemed to go unanswered. Then one day I got a call asking if I would take in a severely retarded seven year old. The Holy Spirit led me to believe this was the "baby" the Lord wanted me to have.

We found out when Nickie came that he was not only mentally retarded but also emotionally disturbed. I knew the Lord had prepared me for this challenge many years before. Nickie was quite a handful! The second week he was in our home he decided to play in the laundry room with the bleach bottle—though he knew he shouldn't. When he heard me coming he ran out of the laundry room and across the entire length of the rec room. By the time I reached him he was quietly sitting down. But I knew exactly what he had been doing because with each step he took the bleach in his socks had bleached all the coloring out of the brand new wall-to-wall carpeting in the rec room. There were permanent reminders of Nickie's dash across the room!

Another trick Nickie had was tearing all his clothes to shreds, particularly his underwear, and flushing them down the toilet. Sometimes these escapades would have our entire plumbing stopped up for a day. He needed 24-hour supervision.

Nickie was so lovable. Everyone who knew him liked him. He was always smiling. We gave him little chores to keep himself occupied—clearing the table, picking up clothes, dressing himself, etc. We were privileged to have Nickie for three years. We finally had to give him up to an institution at the request of his natural parents.

One day we got another call—did we have room for a five-year-old boy and his one-year-old baby brother for just a few weeks? This was just before Christmas. What a present from the Lord! When they came they had only a small paper bag which held all of their earthly possessions. After one year their natural mother wanted to give them up for adoption, but the natural father wanted the kids back. I prayed to the Lord asking why, since the children were not saved, should they be taken from us to go to an unsaved father.

Not long after, the father came and visited. At this point we were resigned to let them go. It is unheard of for the natural father to give up his children after he has had physical contact with them. I prayed along with the rest of the family that the Lord's will might be done—if they were to go back to their natural father we were ready to accept it. I had peace that evening. A week later we got a telephone call. The case worker said, "Mrs. Bailey, I don't know what happened—this has never happened before—but the father is giving up his rights over the children. You can adopt them."

Praise the Lord that He let us have these little boys. They're eight and three now. The older one was classified as retarded. But with prayer, love and a Bible memorization program, he was retested and will now be able to attend normal classes. His IQ was raised 50 points within six months after the Bible memorization program began!

Theresa, a 14-year-old girl, joined our family a year and a half ago. She will be entering high school in September. She has also accepted the Lord as her personal Savior.

Over the years we have also had temporary kids. We

had a 12-year-old blind girl for three months, two 14-year-old girls about three weeks and a 17-year-old boy for two months for a total of 20 children that passed through our house, including the ones we have now. I have also baby-sat for about 21 children over the years, including two I am now baby sitting for.

Little did I realize at the age of 18 that I would travel all the way to America, learn about the Lord Jesus, and be used by Him in this way. I pray that the Lord might continue to use me for His service. Our home is always open to children. When the telephone rings with a "can you take this child?" I feel it is the Lord calling me to take in one more of His little ones.

4 / The King's Daughter Is All Glorious

JoAnn Harvey

With all the talk today about abortion we have often thought of our three adopted children and how glad we are that their lives were not "aborted." How thankful we are that God has allowed us to love and appreciate our children as His special gifts to teach, humble and instruct us in His ways.

Like most married couples Bob and I talked about and planned for the day when we would have a family. My husband used to tease me and say, "I want enough children so that I have to count them to keep track of them." We talked and dreamed and waited. The first three years were busy ones—Bob was attending seminary and I was a working wife. So we planned for the family that we were sure God would give to us.

Our first church was in a small town in Iowa, and as we began our new ministry we were also hoping that we could have our first baby. The next few years were active ones but became increasingly frustrating for me. My emotions were in constant fluctuation. Sometimes I felt confident that God was going to answer our prayers for a child. At other times I felt that for some reason He was turning His back on our request. Little did we know that God was going to give us children but not in the way we had planned.

After two years of going to doctors, trying to become pregnant, praying and pleading with God, Bob and I began to talk about the possibility of adopting. I've always felt that adoption entails the same love-trust relationship of husband and wife as natural childbirth. We had long talks about our feelings concerning adoption. My husband is a tender and caring man, but I also knew that he wanted, if possible, children born from our union as man and wife. In no way did I want to disregard his feelings. It seemed necessary that we both feel comfortable with the idea of adoption. As we talked, two things became apparent. We did not want anything that God did not want for our lives, and we felt that we could both love, sacrifice and take full responsibility for adopted children. Like most adoptive parents our thoughts were not in terms of doing something wonderful for this child, but rather we felt the blessing would be ours and that God would teach us much about ourselves, our dependence on Him and how to give of ourselves unselfishly. We were anxious for this particular experience of love.

After five years of marriage we began the adoption procedure. Many people in our church were helpful and encouraging as we began the long wait. Others gave us dire predictions concerning the unknown backgrounds of adopted children. I remember one day countering with, "I believe the best thing about adoption is that the child will be free from all my inherited faults and failings, and that can only be a bonus!"

In January of 1958 we received a letter telling us our baby son could be picked up on the 22nd. The excitement and anticipation of that moment would be repeated twice more at two-and-a-half year intervals, with our next two children being girls. When the appointed day finally arrived to pick up little Michael Robert, I could hardly wait to get into the car and take him home with us. When he started crying the minute we pulled away from the curb I thought, "Now what do I do?" Parenthood was here—all six pounds of it—and we were a little frightened of the prospects.

Being adopted by two people who want you very much is one thing but being adopted by a whole church is another. The people in our small congregation showered us with gifts of all kinds and still think of our children as partly belonging to them.

When Lynn arrived in 1960 she was like a small "cupie" doll with a brown curl right down the middle of her head and large, beautiful green eyes. Mike took one look at her and told her she was the nicest sister he ever had! A few months later she was crying in her crib in the living room. As I stepped to the kitchen door to see what was the matter I saw Mike peering down into his sister's red face and in a disgusted voice saying, "You sure are crabby." I think these two conflicting emotions continued throughout their growing up time.

In 1963 our second daughter, Laurie, arrived. She was the largest of our babies and the healthiest. Michael has been bothered with allergies of many kinds and Lynn, premature at birth and having a twin who died of respiratory failure, had a lot of catching up to do as far as weight was concerned. With the arrival of Laurie we felt that God had indeed answered our prayers and had given us our family.

I'm sure that Christian women who carry their babies in their wombs for nine months are very conscious of that new life within. They are in constant prayer for a

safe delivery and a healthy baby. Even more, they pray
that God in tender mercy and love will bring this child to
know Himself as Savior and Lord. The same was true of
us. Long before our children came we began to pray for
them. We have always had two goals for our children:
that they come to know Christ Jesus as Savior, claiming
His forgiveness of sins; and that they also know Him as
Lord of their lives, trusting Him to guide them in all His
ways. Believing in a sovereign God who had not allowed
us to have children by the normal process, we accepted
His sovereignty in the choice of those children He allowed us to raise and nurture for Him. I remember
looking into the baby faces of each of my children and
praying, "Dear God, this is Your special gift; remind me
that they belong to You." I didn't know the ways in which
God was going to do just that!

From an early age we read to the children, played with
them, prayed with them, sang to them and enjoyed
them. I remember Mike as a little boy saying to one of his
playmates one day, "This is my Mom. We have fun together." I still cherish that compliment.

Life in a Pastor's home means busy schedules for both
parents, lots of people around and continually going to
church meetings. Our children adjusted to all of these
things and seemed to enjoy the attention they received
from our church family. There were always lots of playmates at the church picnics and socials. We are glad that
they started their lives knowing the love and caring spirit
of our small congregations in Iowa. Families were always
sitting together in morning worship services. Sometimes
we would hear a dad or a mom clomping down the stairs
at the back of the sanctuary. We knew that after proper
discipline had been applied to the proper place, they
would return and the children would sit quietly through

the rest of the service. This included the pastor's children as well.

Our family vacation times are a yearly highlight. When the children were small we rented cabins at various lakes and thoroughly enjoyed fishing, boating and swimming. We've traveled to many parts of the United States and seen many interesting sights. As the children grew older we discovered Mount Hermon, a Christian family conference center in California. Every summer we would ask the children, "Where do you want to go this time?" They would reply without hesitation, "Mount Hermon." It became our special place.

From earliest childhood we were careful to tell the children that they were adopted. We didn't want this to come as a surprise to them. They in turn have repeated the information to others, sometimes for shock value, sometimes to gain sympathy or sometimes just to prove their special worth! Whatever their motive it's their story to tell. Our children have approached their adoption in different ways—from ignoring the fact by not asking questions, to fantasizing about the parents that might have been, to "someday I may go out and look for them." In each of these instances we have tried to put ourselves in their shoes. We pray that God will help us to look on their questioning not as a personal rejection but as a natural response. We pray that God would help us not to over-react but to continue to assure them of our love and understanding. One day Laurie said to us, "The kids at school think being adopted is something really special; they don't know it's just ordinary!"

Being adopted doesn't seem to be as big a hurdle for the children as being a P.K. (preacher's kid). One day when Mike was small, Bob saw him hit another boy and knock him down. He called Mike in to see what precipitated the fight. Mike replied, "Well, he was picking on me and said I couldn't do anything about it because I was a preacher's kid. So I showed him what I could do." One of the children complained to us one day that being a preacher's kid meant people expected you to be perfect. We have never tried to hold up false standards for our children to follow. Whatever is said in the Bible about conduct is said not just to preachers, preachers' wives or preachers' children, but to all believers. A sheltered life is hardly possible for preachers' kids. Our children have repeatedly been included in the struggles and successes of other families and individuals by unavoidably being "on the scene" of a pastor's work. Much of our spiritual growth as a family has come from praying together for others and from the years of friendship that grows out of the crowded world of the pastorate.

When our children reached the teen years God was still reminding us of the fact that they belonged to Him. All of our children came to know Christ as Savior at an early age. As Mike entered his teens we could see where his will was often in conflict with the will of God. One summer as we went to Mount Hermon it seemed that through the messages given at the conference God kept telling me that I could not be the Holy Spirit in Michael's life and to let Him do His work of sanctification. Through a crisis caused by the loneliness and insecurity involved with moving to a new community midway in his Junior year of high school, we saw our son give over his will to God. But not without pain and humbling on our part as well as his.

Both in such crises and in the normal frustration of family growth we have been thankful for Christian friends that God has used to help us and our children. One year Lynn, who was then in junior high school, was going through a particularly hard time getting along with a certain girl. During a summer camp experience she had a long talk with her counselor who was of great help to Lynn. Their friendship continued through letters exchanged over the next year.

Growth is impossible without communication and interaction. In our home we have treasured those "bull sessions" with our children concerning their feelings about themselves, each other, their aspirations and dreams and especially their relationship with God. Communication sometimes breaks down. But the willingness to say, "I'm sorry, I was wrong" is something we've always tried to practice. Sometimes we've said it to the children and sometimes they've said it to us. One day when the girls were having a particularly bitter name-calling fight, we decided to air all the grievances. Each could tell what was bothering her about the other and also what she appreciated in the other. By the time their talk was finished they were laughing and telling each other why they wouldn't want anyone else as a sister!

One of the delightful things about adopted children is their different personalities and temperaments. As a child, Mike was gregarious, curious, friendly and in constant motion from morning to night. Talking came early, and once he started there was no stopping him. He had a million questions which dad patiently tried to answer over and over and over. He liked school and wanted to excel. He also liked sports and took part in many different school activities. Lynn was a happy little girl with big expressive eyes and soft brown hair. She was a dreamer, and concentration in school came hard for her. She was a champion of special causes and took on all kinds of projects, especially ones to do with animals. She was definitely a "doer." She liked drawing, macramé, embroidery and was happiest when she was cleaning fish tanks, nursing a wounded pigeon back to health or planning a backyard program for neighborhood children. Laurie was quiet and shy with strangers. When she was small she wanted to be wherever Mike and Lynn were. Whereas Lynn was a "drop it and leave it there" person, Laurie was a "pick it up and put it away" person. If anyone wanted to know where anything was, we asked Laurie. She loves music and is a dependable and capable person.

Last year God was again to say, "They are Mine." He said it by taking our daughter Lynn home to be with Him. It was early Sunday morning, after a special Saturday outing together topped off with a giggle-filled bedtime family discussion. Just before time to be awakened to dress for church, Lynn's heart stopped. She had not been ill, and the autopsy showed there was no apparent cause of death. Lynn was our freckled-faced "sunshine" girl. Her death was a tremendous blow. She and dad were especially close, sharing the same love of animals and doing many things together. He could become impatient with her indecisiveness, but she could usually make him see her side of the story. She had filled our lives for sixteen years with her often stubborn, but so compassionate nature. She loved children and spent much of her free time baby sitting and playing with the neighborhood kids. Lynn loved the Lord and often tried to share her faith with friends at school and with little children she took care of. I remember the day she brought her little sister to me. Holding tight to her hand she said, "Mom, Laurie wants to have Jesus come into her heart." To which Laurie nodded a vigorous "yes" with every curl bouncing.

Because God spared her life at birth we felt that He had given her to us for special love and care. In my sorrow I found myself asking, "Why now Lord, after all these years. She has filled our life so full of joy. Why now?" The answer came from John 6:40. "Give thanks, she's my child and you will see her again," it seemed to say to me. Bob was given comfort unexpectedly by the words of Psalm 45:13-15, *NASB*, "The King's daughter is all glorious within. . . . She will be led to the King . . . into the King's palace." Again, God was reminding us both that she was His child sent into our lives to help us learn to love Him as she did.

During times of crises family members can be drawn closer together in love and appreciation of one another. Our two children, Michael and Laurie, gave us great comfort and help during those pain-filled days. Michael's voice lifted in prayer for us and for God's blessing even though his pain was as acute as ours. Laurie's concern over our well being was shown in thoughtful acts of kindness beyond expectation for a grieving 13 year old. She expressed her own special kind of sensitivity. Remembering Lynn's love of the color blue, she chose a "just right" bouquet of blue flowers to be her "see you later" gift at the cemetery.

Sitting together, holding hands during the funeral service, peace filled our hearts as a family united in the Lord Jesus Christ. We had hope which nothing could take away.

The prophet Jeremiah says, "It is not in man who walks to direct his steps" (Jer. 10:23, *RSV*). We could not foresee the trials and the triumphs. But in and through them all God has been faithful and continues to be so, to us and yes, to those "chosen children" He has given us.

5 / I Have Fast Sneakers

Carolyn Nystrom

I chose a hyperactive child.

Not that I planned it that way. My seven years as a second grade teacher had given me lots of opportunity to see hyperactive behavior on display. I remember particularly one boy who spent all day acting like a two-legged bongo drum. But I could heave a sigh of relief at three o'clock and send him home. If anyone had told me then that I'd soon be on the receiving end of that 3 P. M. farewell, I think I might have avoided all children forever.

But no one told me.

So when I retired from teaching to get settled into a new house and spend more time with our two girls, my husband and I also applied to become foster parents. It seemed a reasonable step. For the first time in our marriage, I was home all day. We had an extra bedroom. We knew that many children needed a temporary place to live. And foster children were "temporary." If it didn't work out, the arrangement would eventually end.

But not all of our foster children would be temporary. Nobody told us that either. But God knew.

All of this was before we met Randy. Randy is a brown-haired, blue-eyed, five-year-old bundle of energy with a smile that bursts its way through the dozens of daily jams he gets himself into.

He can send a dinner table full of people into gales of laughter when he finds the parent-prompted, "Say thank you, Mrs. Glasser, for the nice lunch," too difficult and comes out instead with an enthusiastic, "Thanks, Glass!"

He can become friends at a train station with a perfect stranger by escaping from his father's firm hand clasp, racing over to a grease-smeared railroad worker with the inquiry, "Have you been playing in the dirt?"

He can win a disciplinary reprieve when his teacher reminds him for the 14th time, "Randy, we can't run in the hallway," by shouting over his shoulder, "But I have fast sneakers!"

In the endless hours of medical and educational advice I've received about the cause and treatment of hyperactivity, I haven't found a better explanation.

Sneakers notwithstanding, there is a medical definition. It is also called "hyperkinesis" and refers to an unusual degree of physical action, not directed toward a specific goal. The hyperactive child has great difficulty concentrating because he is distracted by the slightest interruption. Most hyperactive children are of normal intelligence, but they may have a wide range of learning disabilities preventing them from doing well in school.

Our Randy has some loss of auditory perception. That means that his ears hear, but his mind may not understand. One of his teachers says that a child who has this problem listens to the world as if someone were constantly twisting the dial on a radio. He gets bits and pieces, but rarely the whole thing.

And hyperactivity is common—even more common

among chosen children than in the general population. Dr. J. Gordan Millichap, a pediatric neurologist who specializes in the treatment of hyperactive children, says that 4 percent of children under age 12 are hyperactive. Yet, in his practice, 12 percent of his patients are adopted children. If other variables are equal, this suggests that one out of eight adopted children is hyperactive. Of these hyperactive children, 60 to 80 percent will be boys.

Why the high incidence of hyperactive behavior among adopted children? Dr. Millichap is not certain. But he suggests that children who are unwanted by their natural mother are more likely to receive poor prenatal or postpartum care. This can result in brain damage, a possible cause of hyperactivity.

Our own Randy was born to a malnourished mother who underwent long difficult childbirth. By the time he came to us as a foster child three months later, he had survived near starvation and multiple fractures.

And survive he did, through innumerable illnesses and a host of bumps and falls. With his kind of start in life, we knew permanent damage was likely. That he can run and climb and laugh and learn is a testimony to God's work in his body. Hyperactivity was one of the less serious possible outcomes.

But we were warned about it from the beginning. When Randy was an infant, it was all I could do to hold him on the examining table so that our pediatrician could check him. The doctor suggested "unusual degree of activity" but I passed it off with, "Well, he *is* a boy."

When Randy was two, our doctor mentioned it again, but I reminded him of the "terrible two's syndrome" and said I hoped he'd be better by age three. The doctor said he hoped so too, but he rather doubted it would happen.

Randy became available for adoption that year and we

added him to our family of two girls and Craig, another adopted foster child, only 10 months younger. Even though doctors later diagnosed Randy as falling into the highest category of hyperactive behavior, we do not regret that decision—at least not often.

But one hyperactive child in a home does create serious pressures. Randy seems to always move at top speed and talk at top voice. Watching television, reading or carrying on a conversation is next to impossible with him in the room. If I have a cup of coffee in my hand, it is certain to be upset by an unpremeditated but exuberant hug. Lamps are overturned almost daily. Scratched walls, nicked doors, broken toys, torn books—all are a part of family routine. Another child might play with a toy for five years; in Randy's hands it falls apart in moments.

Needless to say he (and therefore we) are welcomed into very few homes. Most people hesitate to say, "Please come for an adults-only evening," which, by the way, would delight us and give us a needed break. Baby sitters don't jump for joy either when we call. A result is that Roger and I often meet in the doorway for a "changing of the guard," each of us having formed separate interests and activities. A few brave teenage souls do venture into our house. On those occasions, Roger and I usually choose to have an inexpensive dinner and spend the rest of the evening in a quiet library. It may seem a curious night out to some observers, but it suits us fine.

The most difficult part of any day is dinner time. Randy becomes more hyper as the day progresses. By evening, I'm tired and rattled by the schedule complications of chauffeuring the girls to various clubs and lessons and then dashing in to prepare dinner. Randy is going full tilt at his daily peak of activity. I'm ready to fall into bed, and there are still four hours left in the day.

I'm probably the only mother of a five year old in the whole world who still uses a toddler gate. But I absolutely forbid any child to set foot in the kitchen while I'm making dinner. And I've only recently softened that rule to the extent that they may enter one at a time—and then only to help with the work.

The hardest time is yet to come. Though I love him dearly, Randy is no joy at the dinner table. On many occasions, Roger and I have each (or both) decided that we weren't hungry after all and simply left the scene of chaos. The girls grab a plate and head for their room. Randy and Craig eat alone and we shovel up the debris later. By that time, we're both too tired and irritated to eat so we try it again at breakfast.

We've tried many solutions to this dinnertime hassle: Randy can eat before we do and wait in his room while we eat; we can eat first and he can wait in his room until we finish; or all four children can eat together with parents eating at nine or ten o'clock—if we still have the energy and desire by then. All of these solutions keep our family from being together during the one meal when we're all in the house. So we usually tough it out and try to make dinner a family occasion. But I won't pretend it's easy or fun.

Other family complications arise from what some experts call "the eggbeater effect." One hyperactive child can soon have all the others stirred into his own behavior patterns. In our family, this shows up most in Craig. Craig is younger than Randy and, left to himself, he is a quiet, almost hesitant little boy. But when the two boys are together, Craig becomes a part of Randy's fast boisterous play patterns. Only an expert could observe them at play and know that Randy is hyperactive and Craig is not. It's no wonder that hyperactive eggbeaters are not welcomed in well-ordered school classrooms. But in spite of the many years I sought to create such well-ordered classrooms, I'm glad that our two boys are together. They are good buddies. It's as if they know that God gave them each other.

There are helps for hyperactive children—medical helps, educational helps and just plain practical ways of organizing a home around a hyperactive child. God has provided many of these aids for Randy.

Most hyperactive children can be helped by medication. This treatment can begin as early as age three or four. There are many available drugs, but the one most commonly used is Ritalin. Eighty-four percent of the children treated with it have increased control of behavior. Ritalin is not a tranquilizer. Quite the opposite. Doctors now believe that Ritalin stimulates the concentration abilities of hyperactive children. Once they are able to keep their thoughts centered on one subject at a time, they are less distractible and their purposeless activity decreases.

Randy can concentrate on TV only if he has recently taken Ritalin. Even then, he moves his chair very close to the screen—his own effort to minimize distraction, an idea he picked up when he was only two. But Ritalin does produce side effects. Dosage must be carefully balanced with body weight. And the body can form tolerance so that the drug is no longer effective. To keep Randy from developing tolerance to Ritalin, he is allowed only 10 tablets per week spread out two per day for five days. This gives him about 40 hours when he is able to calm down and work more or less normally. His doctor monitors his progress every four or five months with a battery or neurological and educational tests to be sure that the dosage is correct and that side effects do not become serious problems.

Together, Randy and I make the hour long commuter train trip to Chicago for these tests. I'm convinced that no mother has lived life to its fullest until she has boarded a deadly silent commuter—where each businessman's head is buried in his own newspaper—with a hyperactive child in hand. Randy admires everyone's tie, lifts a few hats, and greets each new arrival with, "Hi! I'm Randy Nystrom. What's your name?" I alternate between wanting to crawl under a rear seat and pretend that somebody else's kid accidently boarded the train alone and chuckling over the reaction of reserved businessmen shocked out of their morning routine.

An alternative to drug therapy is various food elimination diets. Dr. William Grant Crook and Dr. Ben S. Feingold have each developed such diets. Some children appear to respond well to one or the other of them. A few parents supplement the diet with massive dosages of various vitamins. Adequate medical tests to determine the acceptability of these diets to the general medical community have not yet been conducted. Initial studies indicate that they are effective for only a few hyperactive children.

We tried various diets for Randy and found them expensive, time consuming and all but impossible to follow since labeling of ingredients is not required for many foods. After several months, we and our doctor agreed that Randy's behavior was unchanged.

One truth that has come back to me again and again is that God does not give us a job to do without also providing the resources necessary to get the job done. This has become abundantly clear in Randy's education. Illinois—along with many other states—demands that school districts provide special education for handicapped children—beginning when they are three years old.

Since a hyperactive child usually has accompanying learning disabilities, he is often eligible for these programs. Our own school district has a special education program of this sort, but it is not well publicized. It was only by what would appear to be the most improbable accident that I learned of its existence. Randy was tested and immediately accepted.

The district provides door-to-door transportation, a specially equipped classroom, a master teacher and full-time aid for this small group of seven children. Randy attends school four mornings a week. His teacher comes to homes for conferences on the fifth morning.

God even provided special helps within the special school. Randy is highly distractible. His classroom "just happens" to be adjacent to a small timeout room. The plain walls and closed door of this stimulus-free room make an ideal place for Randy to come with his teacher for individual instruction.

Because Randy has a loss of auditory perception, his speech is quite garbled. His teacher "just happens" to be a specialist in speech therapy. She is also one of the most capable teachers that I have met in all of my years in education.

Randy has some problems with large motor coordination. His doctor suggested swimming lessons. The school "just happened" to introduce weekly swimming as a regular part of the program when Randy entered.

It may look like a lot of good things just happened for Randy. But I know that God brings about His good through these kinds of circumstances.

Though I've been mother to a hyperactive boy for five years, I'm far from expert on how to do the job well. But I have gathered a few suggestions along the way. Here are a few:

1. A gentle hug and a soft voice goes a long way. There is great temptation to keep raising the noise level of conversation in order to compete with Randy's noise. Yet, he should notice that not everyone operates at a yell.

2. When I am giving him instructions, it helps to take his face between my hands and be sure that I have eye contact with him. I usually begin with "Look at me" or "Listen to me."

3. Randy is a blanket lover—he's worn out several. This is a great help since he's likely to feel more calm holding his blanket than at any other time. I've encouraged this and have no desire for him to outgrow it. At least not yet.

4. I use a "naughty chair." (His teacher calls it a "learning chair.") This can be a punishment or simply a method of breaking his momentum of activity. I usually hand him his blanket and set the timer for 10 minutes. Just enough time for both of us to catch our breath.

5. I also use his bedroom as a timeout room. I can go there with him and close the door to be alone. Or I can send him there to play "until he feels more quiet," again with the door closed. Of course, his room is stripped of breakables.

6. Hyperactive children develop a negative view of themselves very quickly. I try to praise him whenever possible and still be honest. But I don't hand out verbal lollipops for free. He has to earn them.

7. Perhaps the most difficult day-to-day decisions I have to make are in the areas of discipline. It would not be good for Randy if I let him run wild excusing all wrongdoing with, "Well, he *is* hyperactive." On the other hand, he really is not able to control his behavior in a way that other children can. Roger and I have tried to develop some consistency in what we expect from him,

the consequences of transgression, and to mix the whole recipe with a large dollop of hugs and kisses. But the outcome is far from perfect.

In spite of good intentions, I often fail to follow even our own well-planned program. Impatience and anger take over. There are shouts, blows, locked doors. Sometimes depression and a sense of failure beats me down.

Randy, himself, has helped me at those times. When he was three, he began to learn the song, "Jesus Loves Me" in Sunday school. He never got any more than two or three words in proper sequence, but I recognized brief snatches of the song. Then he did something wrong. I've forgotten what. I yelled and ranted and threatened. He was subdued for a moment, then grinned up at me, "Jesus loves me when I'm bad."

He's probably forgotten the incident by now, but it stuck with me, and I'm as likely to apply it to myself as to him.

Do I have regrets? Yes, sometimes. But more often, I'm glad that Randy has joined our family. His life would have been difficult regardless of where he grew up. I like to think that it is less difficult than it might have been.

Even in our worst moments, I hang on to the fact that God brought us together. And a sovereign God doesn't make mistakes—even when He brings to a quiet, scholarly, school-teacherish family, a little boy who can't stop running because he has fast sneakers.

Technical information from, *The Hyperactive Child with Minimal Brain Dysfunction,* J. Gordan Millichap, M.D., YearBook Medical Publishers, Inc., Chicago, London, 1975. Pages 1, 4, 5, 10, 115-117.

6 / One Parent...
Better Than None*

James C. and Marti Hefley

Since this article first appeared, the availability of children for single-parent adoption has sharply decreased. In fact, except among blacks it is practically nonexistent. there are two reasons for this. First, any black or mixed-race children go to black couples or single black parent—not white! About five years ago black case workers met in Atlanta, Georgia, and decided to oppose trans-racial adoption. From that point forward, trans-racial adoption became extremely difficult. The only exceptions made beyond that point were to parents who had already adopted trans-racial children. Secondly, because of abortion, there are very few children carried full term and thus available for adoption. The few that are available for adoption go to couples, not single parents. Miss Simpson has constantly been asked how single people can adopt now. Having checked with Lake Bluff Homes for Children and Chicago Child Care she found that neither of these groups are making white single parent adoptions, and that they know of no agencies that were.

Despite the fact that single-parent adoption is increasingly

*Adapted from *Today's Health* Magazine, March 1971—all rights reserved. Used by permission. Ages and other facts have of course changed since first publication.

more difficult, we felt Miss Simpson's story would help show the changing climate in adoption.

Five years after adopting Anna, Miss Simpson adopted Sarah as a new born. Each child has had her share of medical problems. But this is really what mothering is all about—to help them cope with their difficulties and grow up to be well-adjusted children and young people. Her most difficult problem since becoming a mother has been locating and maintaining baby-sitting arrangements. Miss Simpson looked for a baby sitter that reflected her value system, her Christian commitment, and with a deep love for the children beyond the superficial baby-sitting chores to make the situation really work. God supplied her need at every point along the line, but not without a great deal of concern and searching for just the right person.

Grace Simpson became a mother in 1970 though she's never been married or pregnant. Miss Simpson is one of a small group of persons who have become "single parents" through adoption.

Adoption is the logical step for childless married couples who want youngstes. But back in 1969 there were far fewer husbands and wives applying to agencies than there were children available. Many youngsters were classified as "hard to place" because of race, physical impairment or other reasons. These children often were destined to spend their early years in institutions or in a traumatic series of foster homes.

Single-parent adoption provides an alternative solution to this plight. Sociologists recognize that a stable, two-parent home would be best for any child. But for youngsters who can't wait for this ideal situation to come

along, this is obviously the second-best solution. And for
some single adults who crave the joys of parenthood,
single adoption is the answer to their prayers.

Adoption laws in the United States have long stipu-
lated that a single adult may adopt a child. Until recently,
this was seldom done—except during the Great Depression, when relatively few couples were applying for children, explains Morris Lefkowitz, director of services for
the Children's Home Society of California. "Then in
1965, our state Department of Social Welfare began allowing us to again place some children (for whom two-
parent homes could not be found) with single adults."

Walter A. Heath, executive director for the Los
Angeles County Department of Adoptions (largest of all
such organizations in the United States), accented the
caution his staff followed in beginning their program of
single-parent adoption in late 1965:

"We all agreed that a child needs both a father and a
mother to make the proper sexual identifications and
that two parents are vital for supporting each other psy-
chologically and emotionally in caring for a child. The
only issue ever involved was whether we could find
enough couples. Some of the staff thought we should
work harder to accomplish this goal. I told them, 'If we
can find couples, let's do it. If not, let's get off the dime
and get some single parents. The stability and security
offered by one parent is better than the insecurity of an
institution or a series of foster homes.' "

Los Angeles "got off the dime" by launching a public-
ity campaign to call attention to the need for adoptive
parents, both single and married. Four or five children
were featured each week on an afternoon television program. They represented a group of more than 300 "special need" children: about 275 black or black-and-white

youngsters, 60 Mexican-Americans, 18 children of other mixed racial backgrounds, and several Caucasian and minority group children with severe medical problems.

More than 1800 applications poured in during a three-month period in late 1965 and early 1966. Many of these came from single adults. Within two years, Los Angeles social workers placed 36 of these children with single parents: 35 with women and one with a bachelor. Twenty-one of the women and the one man were Negro; 10 were Caucasian; five were Mexican-American. No discrimination was made on the basis of marital status. Widows, divorcees, and never-marrieds were considered on individual merit.

Welfare departments and agencies in several other states followed California and began inviting single-parent applications for hard-to-place children. The Child Welfare League of America, standard-setter for 300 member agencies in the United States and Canada, encouraged single-parent adoption along the same principle as the program in California—where two parents are not available, then a single parent is the next best alternative.

In questioning leading welfare agencies in New York, Illinois, and California, we found general agreement on the essential qualifications for single-parent adoption. Primarily, the prospective parent must have a realistic and strong desire for a child. The adult also should have previous experience with youngsters. He or she is examined to ensure adequate physical health and emotional maturity. Agencies want the home to provide a healthy sexual environment and companionship for the child, as well as financial security and day care when the parent is working.

The chief requisite is the realistic desire for a child.

Grace Simpson is an ad agency executive who lives in a Chicago suburb. She related her reasons for adoption as she bounced her biracial daughter on her knee: "I realized that my success in advertising was not completely fulfilling. I wanted to transmit myself in terms of human lives. I felt I had every capacity other women have to love a child and be a mother.

"I really thought in terms of what I could do for a baby," she continued. "But Anna has done far more for me than I could possibly do for her. She has brought me into a whole new world. Her responses have given me an unbelievable fulfillment.

"The baby has curtailed some of my outside activities," she admitted. "I am not able to actively serve in my church, and I don't travel as much now. Recently Anna had a bad throat infection and had to be given penicillin. And she's allergic to milk and must have a special formula. Anybody who says a baby isn't taxing hasn't ever raised one."

Miss Simpson's experience tallied with statements of adoption agency representatives: A prospective single parent must realize the responsibility and effort involved in caring for a child.

"We've had many single applicants withdraw when they learned what child care involves," noted Los Angeles County's Walter Heath. "One of our potential single-men placements didn't work out because he had never realized children are a 24-hour-a-day, seven-day-a-week job."

Mrs. Mabel Michaels, a divorcee in her 40's is a self-employed beautician who lives on Chicago's south side. She raised two stepsons before adopting 13-month-old Sherry Lynn.

"After my divorce, I had time on my hands," she recalled. "I felt I could devote myself to something more constructive than just myself. One day I told a customer who is a welfare worker that I would love to adopt a child, but didn't think it possible. She said, 'Oh, I don't know; there's less red tape now. Call this number.'

"I called, and they invited me down for an interview. I was their first single parent. The process was easier than I thought it would be. I know they took into consideration my experience of raising children."

A few blocks away lives another adoptive single mother. She's a divorcee named Mrs. Bess Johnson, a science teacher at a Chicago high school. She already was raising a nephew, George, whom she formally adopted, as well as a six-month-old biracial girl. Commenting on her philosophy on child rearing, Mrs. Johnson said, "I believe in loving a child, giving them what they need and beating their behinds when they're wrong."

She smiled and added, "I knew what I was getting into because I raised George since he was a baby. A few people thought I was foolish to take on another child. But what's life for except to give? There isn't anything I wouldn't do for my children."

A single father, Tony Gallo, of suburban Portland, Oregon, is a piano teacher and music therapist. "I had 70 private pupils, most of them from 6 to 19 years of age, when I adopted my two sons," he said. "So I knew something about kids."

Three years ago, bachelor Gallo adopted Anthony Eric, of Italian-Spanish origins, now six, and Christian William, a Mexican-Indian, now four. "I had so much to give and no children to give it to except my students," he said. "Life is so much richer now."

Adequate health is an obvious necessity for anyone adopting a youngster. Only Grace Simpson of the four single parents with whom we talked has had a serious health problem. Miss Simpson suffered a heart problem for many years until a new drug helped bring it under control.

"I told the agency about my past heart problems," she said. "They required an EKG, which I passed with flying colors."

Agencies also try to determine emotional maturity. Ethel Branham, assistant director of the Los Angeles County Department of Adoptions, points out that records describing single parents frequently note characteristics such as vigor, stamina, patience, understanding, sensitivity, sense of humor, relaxed or level-headed manner. In an article for the U.S. Department of Health, Education, and Welfare's periodical, *Children,* she noted:

"Their willingness to tackle the job of raising a child without the support of a husband suggests that they have a high degree of frustration tolerance. Adoption workers have described them as both self-aware and self-confident—strong enough to accept the likelihood of encounters with those who would imply that the adopted child was a child born out of wedlock and secure enough to handle the innuendo.

"For the most part, they were well-organized, systematic managers. They exhibited good intelligence, although some did not have a good education. They tended to be employed in jobs that gave them opportunities to deal with people rather than with things. Their lives included self-enhancing interests, hobbies, travel, and church or community involvement.

"Their motive for adoption was what they could do for a child rather than what the child could do for them."

Grace Simpson has had her emotional maturity tested by reaction of other people. Her healthy sense of humor showed as she related a few experiences.

"When I went to buy my layette, a saleslady asked me, 'When are you expecting?' I answered, 'Soon, I hope.' 'Well, you sure don't look like it,' she replied.

"The first Sunday after Anna came, a male friend went to church with us. One of the officers asked my girl friend, 'Was it a sudden marriage?' Another person came up to me and gasped, "She's so—so dark, and uh, you're so white." Then he went off mumbling.

"In public places people look at me, my baby, and then my ring finger. You can almost see the wheels turning. We get two kinds of looks—hate and curiosity. When I'm close to people who are staring, I sometimes smile and say, 'Isn't my baby beautiful? She's my adopted darling.' I could wear a ring or have Mrs. put before my name, but I'd feel dishonest. I don't want Anna to someday think I was ashamed because of her."

What about relatives and friends? "My widowed mother and two brothers have helped me from the start. So have people at the office. But . . ." she paused, "to be honest, I must say some people have been blunt in expressing their disapproval. I've had remarks from whites such as 'Is this the best you could get?' and 'Can you take her back?' A few blacks have told me, 'You wouldn't want us raising your white children.'

"I anticipated adopting a biracial or black child, since these are about the only ones available to singles," Miss Simpson said. "A social worker counseled with me about handling prejudice. It was easy to give all the answers intellectually. But after becoming Anna's mother, I found I was hurt by unkind remarks about the baby. Fortunately, my social worker was able to offer practical advice. If it hadn't been for her and my faith in God, I don't know what I would have done.

"My inner adjustment to prejudice has taken time," she continued. "I only hope I will be able to help somebody else who may face the same reactions."

Bess Johnson also noted a few unpleasant reactions to her biracial adoption because of her baby's lightness.

"I got comments like, 'Maybe you should have taken one a little more . . .' A little more what? What difference does it make? This baby is as much a child of God as anyone else."

Healthy interpersonal relationships are another area that adoption agencies examine in prospective parents. Dr. L. M. Luczy, consulting psychiatrist for the Los Angeles County Department of Adoptions, stressed, "We always look for the possibility of homosexuality or lesbianism. We can't take a chance on having a child abused sexually.

"We are also concerned about previous marriages, but this doesn't rule out divorced persons. A woman may have been married to an inadequate man and be quite capable of motherhood. We are concerned about the possibilities of remarriage. We don't want a man, for example, who is not interested in marriage."

Grace Simpson recalled how the agency psychiatrist "questioned me about why I wasn't married and what my attitude is toward men."

The new environment should provide a heterosexual identity for the child. Agency representatives readily conceded that this is the ground for a major objection to single adoption. However, we were reminded that thousands of children are already growing up in homes where one parent is absent because of separation, divorce, or death.

Dr. Benjamin Spock said in a discussion on the fatherless family: "The remarkable thing is that he [a young

child] can create a parent who will serve many of his
needs if he has to. . . . Of course a real father . . . will be a
lot more satisfactory than an image, on many scores. But
if there isn't a real one, the mother's job is not to try to be
one . . . but to maintain a wholesome environment for
the child so that he can create a wholesome one in his
imagination."

"It is very important," Doctor Luczy asserted, "that a
child adopted by a single woman have the opportunity of
male companionship." Records in the Los Angeles Department of Adoption show a wide assortment of male
identification available for the adopted children of single
women: brothers, fathers, sons by a previous marriage,
nephews, uncles, adult male friends, and in a few cases
even former husbands of the adoptive mother.

Grace Simpson has male business friends. Also, her
brother, who lives a few blocks away, agreed to help
supply a male relationship for her daughter. "Does he
ever!" she exclaimed. "He pitches her up in the air while
I stand by and gasp." Her 12-year-old nephew also
spends after-school hours with the child.

The Oregon music teacher reported he has no problem providing examples of female family members for
his boys. "There's my mother and sister, who live close
by," he said. "And I have a housekeeper and plenty of
female students."

A so-called extended family can be an asset to the
single mother or father. "We want the single parent to
have enough of a family around that the youngster will
get the feeling of a family group and the idea of what a
good marriage may be," explained Dorothea Lane of the
Illinois Children's Home and Aid Society.

"We want to know who will be the backup person or
persons in case the single parent becomes ill," added Ger-

trude Sandgrund, adoption department supervisor at Louise Wise Services in New York.

Each of the four single parents we interviewed have relatives nearby. Miss Simpson also has a lady housemate and her widowed mother living with her.

Each in our quartet of single parents has an adequate income. Miss Simpson is a vice president of the advertising agency. Tony Gallo has his music pupils. Mrs. Michaels has a flourishing beauty shop in her home and believes business has even increased because customers enjoy seeing her daughter. Mrs. Johnson has teacher tenure with the Chicago school system.

"Usually the adopted parent is employed," explains Miss Lane, adoption supervisor of the Illinois agency, "so we insist a care plan be established before we consent to the placement." Mae Neely, supervisor of New York City's Adoption Unit in the Bureau of Child Welfare, observed that "this is the chief problem single men have in adopting children."

Each of our single parents had taken this in mind. Both Mrs. Michaels and Tony Gallo work at home. He has a housekeeper to help with cleaning and cooking.

Mrs. Johnson and Miss Simpson both employ regular sitters, a significant increased expense. Fortunately, some compensation comes from a change in income tax reporting status: A single adoptive parent is classified as head of a household.

"I wanted a sitter I could trust completely without having to call from the office and check on the baby," Miss Simpson said. "My sitter and I have similar values. She has three children of her own plus two adopted Koreans, one of whom is a boy. This gives Anna a brother during the day."

Apparently, single-parent adoption is working well

with the four individuals we interviewed. Grace Simpson is already planning for a second adoption: "a biracial sister for Anna," she said. "Growing up with a white mother and relatives, they could give each other identity support."

The science teacher, Mrs. Johnson, is "thinking of a little brother for my children—just somebody who needs a home."

Mrs. Johnson's pediatrician, Dr. Alice Buckley, expressed her reservations about single-parent adoption. "I'm not sure whether I'm for it in general," she said, "but it seems to be working for this lady."

Miss Simpson's main concern about the future centers on her daughter's acceptance in every phase of community life. "Times are changing, and I hope Anna will be accepted for what she is as a person."

*   *   *

Helpful information about adoption agencies can be obtained from the Child Welfare League of America, which offers services through the North American Center on Adoption, the Adoption Resource Exchange of North America (ARENA)—one program of the North American Center on Adoption—and other service agencies.

ARENA acts as a resource for adoption. Their primary service is to adoption agencies. Prospective parents can call them for information concerning hard-to-adopt children. In some cases these children can be adopted away from local pockets of prejudice. For example, Indian children are wanted in the East, though they are hard to place in the West.

Though single-parent adoption is becoming more difficult and is not possible in all states, it can be meaningful
to both child and parent when it is possible.

Roy Rogers and
Dale Evans (left). Roy
and Dale (below) with
their adopted children,
natural children and
grandchildren.

Cheaper by the half-dozen? Or at least Bonnie and Dennis Wheeler's children have more brothers and sisters to play with. Becky and her "Robby-powered" wheel chair (left). "Look, mom, four hands!" (Timmy and Benji, right). A long couch (below) and a loving home for Julie, Benji, Becky, Robby, Timmy and Alicia (left) to right.)

Diny and Tom Bailey (above) with *most* of their children: (left to right) Marlene, Beth, Maryann, Judy, Angelo, Teddy, Gordon, and Tony (1967). A full house, even with three children away, at a recent family gathering: (left to right) Maryann, Tony, Diny, Donovan, Terry, Judy, Carl, Teddy, Beth and Angelo.

The Harveys share a happy
moment. Lynn, Mike and Laurie
(standing, left to right).
Bob and JoAnn (seated).

Randy and Craig (below right), ready for a "Big Wheel" race. Carolyn Nystrom (left), and husband Roger (below), with their children, Randy, Sheri, Lori and Craig.

Ted and Judy Johnson with their mother "Vi" (right). Elmer Johnson (Ted and Judy's father)—proud of his "big catch"—and his grandchildren, Jeff and Jill.

Ted Johnson with his wife Jerry (far left above) and their children Jill and Jeff. Judy Johnson (far right) with her husband Douglas and their children Joel and Anne.

The Dennis children—Jon, Sasha, Jenay and Geoff (left to right)—stop long enough for a quick picture while hiking in the Arboretum. Ebeth and Lane Dennis (below) with three of their children (1971).

Doris Wheeler (left), Executive Director of the Evangelical Child and Family Agency (ECFA), greets children at the agency's center. ECFA offers a full range of family counseling and other services (below).

7 / "You're Adopted!"

Ted Johnson

Recalling so many fond memories of our dear parents only reaffirms the fact that we were most fortunate to be chosen by them.

I think of the good qualities that each possessed. Dad was strong of mind and stature, ambitious, persistent, helpful, stern when needed, generous, sincere, dedicated, willing and always with a smile on his face and a twinkle in his eye.

Mom was always thoughtful, putting others first and herself last. She was beautiful, willing, uncomplaining, friendly, a dear Christian and a tremendous example to all that knew her.

Looking back on my early childhood, I realize that regarding the subject of my natural parents everything wasn't done exactly according to the book. Nevertheless, my adoptive parents handled it in a beautiful, loving and very meaningful way.

It was in school one day when a couple of my third grade friends informed me that I was adopted. My first reaction was, so what—I really didn't know what that meant. They went on to explain that my mother and father were really not my real parents. I didn't believe them. It just couldn't possibly be true. How was this possible, I wondered. Heartbroken, I remember crying all the way home from school that day, hoping that when I arrived home Mother would assure me that I had heard wrong.

As I burst into the house, Mother and several of her friends were having coffee. The tears began to come again—this time in streams—and I ran into my room. In just a few minutes she was there and wrapped me in her arms. I began to explain what had taken place back on the school playground. She then unfolded the story of my adoption so beautifully and with so much genuine Christian love. Still crying, I said, "But Mommy, I wanted to be born from you." She held me tightly while assuring me that truly they were my parents through the adoption process and that I indeed was sent to them by God. She told me that I had been selected above all other children and most importantly that we were really all God's children. Once again she explained His perfect plan of salvation.

I also remember the "arrival" of my sister Judy and the days preceding it, which now seem quite humorous. Mom and Dad told me that soon I would have a baby sister. I became excited and very anxious to see her. I asked how long it would take and they said, "just a few more days." I thought it was great that they already knew it was going to be a girl.

After waiting what seemed like a month the big day finally arrived, and they brought Judy home. She was so cute she immediately became the star attraction of the neighborhood. It now became apparent that I would have to share my parents' love and affection for the rest of my life. Once again they reassured me with their love and made sure that I was given equal attention.

Our family grew up knowing and feeling a genuine attitude of unselfishness. Mom and Dad always took time to spend with us. Dad gave up his Saturday golf game with his best friends which he had always enjoyed for years. He also quit the company bowling team because he felt it took too much time away from his growing family.

We always looked forward to spending our summers at our cottage in Northern Minnesota. Mom would delight in preparing a delicious meal with favorite foods that would please all of us. Following the meal, she would ask someone to pass the "promise box." We all took one, read it, and passed it on. We learned the Scriptures at an early age. As we children read we stumbled over difficult words, but I felt it was one of the most effective tools in learning the Bible. Today we still use that box. I remember Mother taking her usual three cards, one for her dear sister and one for anyone else who needed to claim a promise for the day.

Dad and I enjoyed all types of sports, both as participants and as spectators. I can't begin to recall the number of hours spent on the beautiful grass parkway which ran in front of our house playing catch. I wonder how many baseballs, gloves, footballs, and basketballs we wore out. Every night after dinner we played several games of table tennis. After our skills became about equal, we began to keep a record of our wins by putting a mark on a scrap of wood after each game. We used up several "scoreboards" and I still have the last one. The final count was Dad 1,004, Ted 983.

In 1973 Mother's health began to fail as her earthly light seemed to grow dim. She leaned a bit more heavily on our arms and her hugs were a little longer. She must have sensed that God's plan for her was to be with Him. She was to enter the hospital for tests to determine the cause of her headaches and dizzy spells. Following an angiogram test, she had a cerebral hemorrhage and passed into eternity and God's presence within a few days. I will never forget the family gathered in prayer around her hospital bed. Good friends joined hands with us as we encircled her bed. One offered a most beautiful prayer to God as we dedicated her at that moment into the Lord's presence. A short time later she drew her last breath.

The funeral service for Mom was an uplifting one in which we celebrated her home-going. As a final tribute and with God's strength and assurance from so many prayers, I sang two of Mother's favorite hymns, "He Giveth More Grace," and "Children of the Heavenly Father." God's grace was sufficient.

God's plan was to call Dad home just 13 months later. A trip to Mayo Clinic revealed cancer, and we all carefully prepared to care for him and love him in still a greater way. Dad apologized often for being such a burden to us, but how little he realized that it was now our privilege to love and care for his needs. Dad had given up a lot in his early days as a father; how could we possibly do less for him now? Judy, a registered nurse, supervised his care at her home in a most loving way, and daily he was surrounded by family, friends and his prized possessions—his grandchildren. In his final days, we held him, assured him of our love and talked about the great times we had had together. As he drew his last breath, we knew the final piece to life's puzzle was complete. He and Mother were now at home with the Lord.

I will be ever grateful for being chosen by my wonderful parents. I am sure that it was a part of God's will and ultimately His perfect plan of salvation for my life. As a result of our parents' Christian love and witness, we and our children have a growing and deepening relationship with Christ. "Who can find a virtuous woman? For her price is far above rubies" (Prov. 31:10).

8 / Chosen Family

Judy Johnson

Adoption means to take by choice into some relationship, or to make one's own, something of which one is not the begetter. A synonym for "adopt" is "embrace," and to me it expresses more personally and emotionally the essence of this relationship. Embrace—to joyfully accept, cherish, love, encircle. To receive readily, to welcome! When put in these words, adoption takes on a fuller, richer meaning. I feel that this is what my parents had in mind when they chose to take Ted and me into their lives. I don't know if they would have put their feelings quite like that, but it was apparent all of their lives that they knew adoption was more than just "taking by choice." "To include as parts of a whole" is what I think they had in mind—to build their whole family.

I was adopted at the age of about 14 months after having spent my first year or so in a foster home and orphanage. It is said that even a child's earliest contacts will affect him in later life. If this is true, and I'm sure it is, I must have had some love and gentle care without fear and withdrawal. Dad used to say that the first time they saw me was at the orphanage. The minute

I laid eyes on him I held out my arms to be taken and he was taken too. From that moment on I had found my family and was home.

I suppose the ideal way for a child to find out about his adoption is to be told by his parents as early as possible. But, as often happens, this wasn't the way I found out at all. I think my folks were waiting for the right time—until I was old enough to understand, but before I found out from someone else. I had heard snitches of conversations and certainly had wondered why the lady next door always said, "The first time I saw you, Judy, you were running around the yard and falling down a lot." I couldn't figure out why she hadn't seen me before that. But, I guess I never really worried about it or cared that much. At the age of eight I wasn't given to pondering things too deeply.

Just about then I started catching on that maybe I was a little different from the other kids. One day during morning recess at school I noticed a couple of my friends whispering and giggling and sneaking funny looks at me. Kids aren't too subtle. I asked what was going on, but they said it was a secret and they couldn't tell me. I was naturally a little curious—actually dying to find out. But rather than lower myself to begging, I said, "OK, forget it," and went back to somersaults and jumping rope. I could hardly sit still after recess because I knew I could worm the information out of Gracie on our way home for lunch. Sure enough, as soon as we started for home I ·began my pitch.

"Hey, Gracie! What have you guys been talking about me for?"

"Can't tell, Jude—it's a secret!"

"How come you know something about me that I don't know?"

"My Mom told me and said not to tell anybody!"

"How come you told Diane, then? If it's about me don't you think I should know? Is it bad?"

"No."

"Why can't you tell me, then?"

"OK. You're adopted!"

There it was! Plunked right in my lap in one big word. *Adopted!* Well, I'd asked for it, but I didn't really know what I had asked for. So rather than appear "uncool" in front of my friend, I just said, "So what!" And she said, "So nothing, I guess. No big deal." That's how the news first came to me that I was different. We never mentioned it again, and we're still friends—30 years later.

At that point I was still "cool" in front of my friend, but inside I was in a turmoil. I didn't even know what the word meant. Eight year olds weren't quite as savvy in those days as they are now. So I ran the rest of the way home thinking terrible thoughts—maybe I had an awful disease or something. I hadn't a clue what the word meant or why it made me different. I certainly looked like any other eight-year-old kid—skinny, knobby, bruised knees, gangly and awkward. All the right parts were there. I even went to Sunday School and took piano lessons like the other kids. If I was different you sure couldn't tell by looking at me!

With that kind of disquiet going on inside of me I burst into the house—panting and wild-eyed, I'm sure. Poor Mother! I think she had always planned how to tell me—perhaps one of those quiet, intimate mother-daughter talks in the right setting. Or maybe she and Dad could have gently broken the news at some opportune time—bedtime, or perhaps on a quiet walk on the beautiful, grassy parkway in front of our home. Well, you know what happens to the best of plans! Here she was with a rather upset young girl on her hands—a first-class emergency! I know she must have prayed a quick, silent prayer, "Lord, help me right now, please!" Then she took me on her lap and told me as simply but completely as she could what it meant to be adopted. She told me that Dad and she loved me as much as if I had been born to them and that I was indeed their own daughter. God had planned it that way for me and for Ted and for them. Now their prayers were answered and their family was at last complete.

I was completely satisfied and especially so relieved to know that I was a regular, normal person. After all, if God had planned this for us, it must be right. And so it always was—just right! We had our ups and downs, of course. Doesn't every family? Growing pains, adolescent trials, cutting the apron strings, and starting out on our own were all a part of our family, too. But, they were the perfect parents for us. They knew just when to hold us back for our own good, and when to let us go—and always, always with love. I think it was because I knew I was loved without reservation that I never needed to know more about my background. Now that I'm grown I do know more; Dad told me all he knew in the last months of his life. Knowing has only made me more grateful for having had an extra blessing that only chosen children have. God has gven me so many blessings in my life. First, the gift of life itself, then the gift of a "chosen family," for he truly chose this special couple and brother for me. Then, best of all, He gave me the gift of eternal life—to be born again as a Christian and be part of an even larger family.

I have also received an extra-special gift that not even most chosen children are given. All my life I had a special friend. We spent our summers together growing up and developing the kind of respect and fondness for each other that builds a firm foundation for a deeper relationship. Doug was my first cousin and never knew, or didn't remember, that I was adopted. It wasn't a secret or anything; it was just an accepted fact and rarely if ever was mentioned. When we were in college, and still good friends, I happened to mention one day that I was adopted. From that time on our friendship grew and developed into love. That was 18 years ago and now we've been married for 15 years and have a daughter and son of our own—very special gifts from God! The Aunt and Uncle I loved as a child are now my parents by marriage—even more dear to me since my chosen parents are with the Lord.

What more could one person have in life? And yet daily God increases his blessings to us. His love is so enormous I hardly know how to express it in words. So I can only try to love and serve Him more and pass it on to the family He chose for me!

PART TWO
THE ADOPTION PROCESS

9 / The View From an Agency

Doris Wheeler

"I remember the evening when . . . ," began a dean at Moody Bible Institute as she related to me an incident that occurred during her student days at Moody. Someone had abandoned a newborn baby in a cardboard carton in the doorway at the Institute. It seemed obvious that whoever left the child wanted her to be placed in an evangelical Christian home. They must have realized that, although there were good agencies in the Chicago area at the time, there wasn't one that would give a 100 percent promise that the baby would be placed in an evangelical Christian home.

Out of that incident and from the concern it aroused, the Evangelical Welfare Agency was formed. The Agency is 26 years old, and under its current name of Evangelical Child and Family Agency, it provides the programs of adoption, foster care, services to unmarried parents and a limited amount of family counseling. The Agency is unique because staff members know Jesus Christ as Lord and Savior and because the homes in which children are placed, either for adoption or foster care, are homes in which the parents have had a personal experience with Jesus Christ.

For the 26 years since that first little baby was found, we have been looking for adoptive homes for infants and older children. Often we are asked by prospective applicants, "What are you looking for in couples?" Some who are reading this book may be contemplating adoption and wondering if they qualify to become adoptive parents. Let me just share a few of the things that we like to see in couples who will become parents.

First of all, we are not looking for perfect couples! I often tell people that we aren't looking for perfect couples because we don't have perfect children to place anyway. There are, however, certain attributes that are important to most adoption agencies as they evaluate applicants.

Some basic requirements of our agency (other agencies have similar ones) are reasonable physical health, a minimum age of 21, two years married and living in the State of Illinois.

Further, we want people with proper motivation, that is, those who want a child for the child's sake. If the request for a child is made to hold a marriage together, or only to furnish companionship for another child or because relatives and friends think it's the "proper" thing to do, motivation would be questioned.

We also need people who are able to give love without expecting a great deal in return. Sometimes a child who has had a traumatic background or has been moved from home to home is not readily able to return love. He may have been so bruised by past experiences that he is afraid to become emotionally close to anyone. It may take months or even years for a child like that to demonstrate affection in the way parents would like. In fact, we hope that our adoptive couples will not have too high expectations in any area. There is great danger in expecting more of a child than he or she is able to achieve. I can think of a number of children who have never been able to please their parents in academic achievement, in developed talents or in physical prowess. Consequently, the parents withheld praise, and the child developed a very low self-concept.

We are looking for people who can individualize children, helping each to develop his own personality, interests and talents. We want a couple who have a sense of right and wrong and are able to positively portray their own value system. In other words, we are not looking for couples where "anything" goes. Instead, we want adults who can pass on concrete guidelines to children and can be consistent in discipline.

It is important to us that a family can have fun together and express open affection to one another. This, of course, is accomplished in different ways and to different degrees, but we do not like to place a child in a home where these characteristics are nonexistent.

The right perspective on money management and finances is important to us. We do not ask that a couple have a certain amount of money in the bank or that their salary reach a given figure. Rather, we are only looking for couples who are financially able to take care of another child. It is much more important to us that the couple is comfortable with their standard of living and that their lives are not improperly motivated by a desire for wealth.

A *growing* marital relationship is attractive to us. I have not yet seen a perfect marital relationship in which there are no rough spots to be worked on. Therefore, it is good to see a couple who recognize the areas for improvement and are working together on upgrading their relationship. This kind of growth necessitates honest communication, so we look for couples who communicate openly with each other and with us. When a husband and wife can discuss their feelings, fears, goals, likes and dislikes and successes and failures fairly freely, they have a head start on maintaining a workable and satisfying marital relationship.

We want couples who have a reasonable number of friends and extend themselves outside their own home. It will be important to a child that he learn to make friends, and it will be his parents who will show him how.

We are looking for people who have reasonable housekeeping standards. The home reflects the people who live in it; disorder and pandemonium may indicate a disorganization that pervades the family.

Couples who are flexible in the kind of child they will take usually make better adoptive or foster parents. If the couple is very selective about sex, age, physical characteristics and health, we begin to wonder how much they really want to give of themselves to a child who needs parents.

Finally, we look for couples who have a reasonable parenting philosophy. We want people who are not overly rigid or overly permissive, who have reasonable knowledge of ways to help a child toward healthy independence..

I hope these requirements do not look too formidable. Most readers will probably meet all or most of them. I have not described here a perfect couple. These are people who make mistakes, sometimes feel inadequate and who seek for added wisdom—just like you. I have taken the time to list these characteristics so that you would know that agencies look for such traits in a family as you would look for if you were placing your child in someone else's home. There is nothing mysterious about what agencies look for—just good, average people, with lots of love and common sense to share with a child.

10 / Choosing an Agency

Doris Wheeler

In looking for a good reputable agency make sure that it is licensed by the State and that it is in good standing with other agencies and institutions within the welfare community. Here in the Chicago area the State Department of Children and Family Services provides information about private agencies, as does the Council for Community Services of Metropolitan Chicago or the Child Care Association of Illinois. Other states have similar child welfare organizations which may be contacted for information about the agency you want to work with.

It is also wise to check into the affiliations of the agency. For instance, the Evangelical Child and Family Agency is a member of, or associated with, the Child Welfare League of America, the Child Care Association, the Chicago Association of Commerce and Industry and the National Association of Evangelicals. Each agency which you contact will be associated with at least one or more such organizations, and it would be good to find out what those are. Get to know the general reputation of the agency you want to use. If possible, visit with some couples who have been served by them.

The competency and educational background of the agency staff should be looked into. In most child welfare agencies some of the staff must hold a masters of social work degree. Other people on the staff may have a BS or BA degree but be supervised by people with graduate social work training. Agencies should readily supply such information.

It is important to know the number of children available to the agency in question. Some agencies are fairly small and may place only five or ten children per year in adoption. Larger ones may be able to serve you more quickly because of the children available to them. Ask for the agency's annual report. Most agencies prepare these. The information includes financial statistics, service statistics and the agency's general philosophy.

There are both not-for-profit and for-profit agencies operating in the field of adoption. Both kinds of agencies can deliver good service, but it helps to be aware of their financial policies and general philosophy.

FEES

Agencies who are heavily endowed or tax supported may not have an adoption fee. Other agencies may have a sliding-scale fee based on income. In some communities fees vary quite considerably. Currently in the Chicago area a reasonable adoption fee may be between $1800 and $2500. We call this reasonable because it costs agencies in this area that amount to complete an adoption. Therefore, a not-for-profit agency could charge that sum and not be making a profit. This fee is usually for professional services and covers casework counseling, home finding, costs for the unmarried mother's care and the child's care before placement. The fee may be payable in different ways, but many agencies will ask for it in payments rather than a lump sum. Information regarding the fee should be readily available from the beginning of contact with the agency. Often it is explained in detail during an orientation meeting before the formal home study begins.

PROCESS OF REJECTION

Many couples have been frustrated when an agency has decided that they could not place a child in the home but have not given a reason for that decision. Policy regarding rejection is determined by each individual agency. Those with a non-disclosure policy probably intend to protect the couple. However, I believe a couple can cope with the truth much easier than with the unknown. Further, if there is some reason which could lead to improvement, the couple can only work on their problem by knowing what it is. The agency's policy on rejections is something that should be found out at the beginning of contacts with them. If an agency rejects a couple's application for a child without telling them why, they still have some alternatives:

1. They might apply to a different agency.
2. They might see a counselor who may be able to discern the reason, especially if it is connected with personality functioning.
3. In some areas, perhaps court action could be taken to insist that the agency give a reasonable explanation.
4. They could, of course, stop their efforts to become parents.

INDEPENDENT ADOPTIONS

While recognizing that many independent adoptions have resulted in a happy family unit with great benefit to the child, many child welfare agencies share a deep concern about the present practice of independent placements. Following are some of the facts which promote that concern:

1. Often the biological parents do not have comprehensive services available to them. These include temporary foster care if they need time to resolve conflicts; adequate counseling which apprises them of alternatives to placement; day care or other facilities which allow alternatives to be implemented; and placement facilities for the infant if he should be born with abnormalities.

2. The biological parents are sometimes coerced into relinquishing the child because an independent arrangement has already been formulated. Thus, there is often no recourse if the mother should return with doubts about her decision.

3. The rights of the biological father are sometimes overlooked or circumvented.

4. The guarantee of confidentiality or privacy for the adoptive family is sometimes lacking.

5. The health and social records kept may be inadequate so that the child may not have proper access to information concerning his origin at the time it is appropriate for him to acquire these data.

6. Presently, exorbitant sums of money are changing hands in many independent adoptions. This leads to the danger that children may be treated as commodities. A child should be placed to serve his best interests regardless of the adoptive parents' ability to pay an adoption fee.

Since protection of children, their biological parents and their adoptive parents is of prime concern to child welfare agencies, all parties stand to gain by working through an agency.

We have had several cases in which independent adoption was not a satisfactory plan. In one instance, a young unmarried mother had agreed to relinquish her baby to a medical doctor and lawyer who were to place the child privately. She worked with them for some months, quite secure in her plan. However, soon before her delivery, the lawyer realized that it was not going to be easy to find the putative father and to get him involved in the relinquishment procedure. When he realized the legal complications, he refused to have anything more to do with the adoption. The young mother came to our agency to see if we could help her. We accepted the case, worked out the legal complications by contacting the putative father and helping him come to a decision regarding adoption and then placed the child in an adoptive home.

On another occasion an unmarried mother was working through a private source toward an independent adoption. The adoptive couple was waiting for the child, and everything seemed to be progressing well until the child was born with a deformity. Suddenly the doctor and lawyer in the independent adoption were no longer willing to carry through the placement. Again, the unmarried mother turned to the agency for placement of her child.

This kind of situation recurs again and again. It results in a troubled unmarried mother and a baby whose placement is delayed, and a potential adoptive couple who are very disappointed because they were waiting for a specific child. In an agency adoption, the adoptive parents are not usually waiting for a specific child. In fact, we wait to do the final matching of the infant until after the baby is born and the mother has signed permanent adoptive consents. That way, there is not an adoptive couple waiting who could be grievously disappointed.

11 / Common Attitudes
   and Fears

Doris Wheeler

Those of you who are contemplating adoption may wonder if your feelings and attitudes are unique to you. To help you see yourselves in perspective, I would like to share a few attitudes and fears which are prevalent among husbands and wives coming to our agency. First of all, it has been my experience that the husband and wife are not usually ready for adoption at the same time. More often it is the husband that is slower in wanting to adopt a child. One of the reasons is that the husband's masculinity is often threatened by the fact that he and his wife cannot have a child naturally born to them. Sometimes the husband has the feeling that somebody else is really giving his wife a child.

There is a second reason that husbands, in particular, seem to hold back from adopting: fear of not being able to love another's child. I have heard husbands express the thought that "somehow it just won't work out." Recently, I studied a young couple where the wife was very anxious to adopt but the husband, in fact, told me that he did not want to adopt. His wife, knowing him well, felt that once a child was placed he would become a very accepting, loving father. Neither the wife nor our agency pushed this man into adoption—that would have been wrong.

As we met in successive interviews some of the man's fears were worked through. Yet, even at the time of placement he was still somewhat leary of taking "another's child." Today, only months after this little boy was placed, this man has become very comfortable with adoption and is a very involved, proud father. This phenomenon is not uncommon. It is important to note, however, that an agency would not place a child if one partner wanted a child and the other partner continued to be against the plan.

Another common fear of applicants is that they won't make it. Let's face it, none of us likes to be judged. Some couples fear they will not be approved and often view the home study as an interrogation. They may see the social worker as a strict investigator. That may be the tone of some studies in some agencies. However, I don't believe it is the prevalent feeling demonstrated by adoption personnel. My philosophy of a home study is that we must become well enough acquainted with a family that we are comfortable in giving a child to them "for keeps." The best way to become well acquainted is to ask the couple to tell us how they function in various areas of their life and their relationship. This is not unlike a family preparing their will and looking for a couple to name as guardians. In so doing that family chooses a couple they know quite well and evaluates that couple's acceptability.

Most of the couples who apply to our agency are eventually approved for placement of a child. We do say "no" to approximately 10 percent of applicants, but in each of those cases we try to help the couple resolve problems so that they might adopt later on. Sometimes we refer them for counseling outside our agency, sometimes we can offer the counseling necessary. Occasionally, there is a family that we believe is not ready for placement and where counseling may not be the answer. We do our best to explain why we think it would be best for them not to adopt.

A third fear is that the child may be from bad stock. This is a feeling that an adoptive couple will have to resolve since agencies often do not know a great deal about the background of a child. In fact, if the child is abandoned, literally nothing may be known about the parents. In other cases, the agency may have had a long-term relationship with and know a great deal about the child's parents, including health history, drug usage, intellectual ability, talents and so forth. This is a subject dealt with during the home study, and couples are usually able to resolve their feelings regarding this issue. Fears regarding heredity are fairly common. But they are probably out of proportion and not nearly as valid as people have been led to believe.

Another feeling is hostility in having to be studied. Often I hear comments like, "natural parents don't have to go through this." What the couple is really saying is that they are uneasy about being evaluated or having their way of living questioned. It has been my experience that a majority of couples, once accepting the necessity, have found the study to be a helpful, learning experience. The success of the study depends very much upon the attitude that one has in entering it. If couples could look at it as an opportunity for growth and gaining knowledge in an area that may have some surprises for them, I believe they would find it a much more exciting, dynamic experience. The philosophy I shared a bit earlier might be a good one to remember in understanding the necessity and reasonableness of an agency's evaluation of a family.

Sometimes a couple may not really be hostile about the procedure of a home study but just may be unfamiliar expressing their feelings about their marriage. It is not always an easy thing to sit down and share your innermost emotions with others, and for the first or second interview it may be an uncomfortable experience. However, if the social worker is skilled and is an accepting person, he or she will be able to help you verbalize adequately. Again, you may find this to be an experience which you enjoy and from which you grow. I have often had a couple talking with me who suddenly turn to one another and say, "I didn't know that," and enjoyed discovering new things about one another in the process of the home study. So, if you are contemplating adoption, I trust that you will not unduly fear the procedure but look forward to it as an opportunity to know one another better and to become prepared for adoptive parenthood. As you begin to realize that your feelings are not unique, adoption will become less of a formidable prospect.

12 / Placing Older and "Special Needs" Children

Doris Wheeler

Often when a family thinks of adopting a child or becoming foster parents they think of accepting an infant or a cute toddler. But there are many other children available for placement all around the country. Our agency emphasizes finding homes for school-age children, ranging from 6 to 12 or 13 and for children with special medical or emotional problems. I would like to challenge the Christian community to consider opening its homes and hearts to these boys and girls who need a family just as much as the younger, more attractive children. Who should be better able to tackle the more difficult placements than Christians who have the strength, wisdom, comfort and peace of the Lord to draw upon?

In the State of Illinois, there are literally hundreds of "special needs" children available for adoption. We have an Adoption Listing Service which provides agencies with the pictures, names and needs of these children. Through this and other means, agencies work together to find appropriate homes as soon as possible. Some of the children that we have placed have had hearing problems, have been crippled or have been hard to place because there were two or three siblings who needed to be placed together. Minority race children, slow learners, and children with chronic illnesses are also among the more difficult to place. Sometimes these children are first placed in a foster home and may be adopted by the foster parents if that is the most appropriate plan. There is often no fee for the adoption of "special needs" children. Moreover, funds are sometimes available for a subsidized adoption in cases where there is undue financial stress.

Older children, too, often require special care. Many have habits which are difficult to tolerate and behavior which must be modified. Sometimes this is in the form of rebellion, bad language, poor discipline, aggressive behavior or isolationism. This behavior may come from insecurity over past placements, fear, abuse or repeated rejections. Though this is true, there is special blessing in meeting the challenge of these behavior patterns and being involved in the problem solving. This is not done through demanding reformation but leading in it.

We had a young teenage boy who came into foster care from a home where the mother had left and the father was an alcoholic. The boy was accustomed to bad language, stealing, skipping school and other behavior not common to the foster family. One day this boy stole an article from a local filling station. After finding this out, the foster father went with the boy to return the merchandise and ask forgiveness of the owner. The boy was so impressed by the example and assistance of the foster parents that it cemented the relationship between "father" and "son" and led to changes in behavior.

Another boy was placed with us at age nine. His mother had abandoned him and other siblings and the boy had seen his father tragically burned to death in their home shortly before coming to our agency. A Christian family who already had four children of their own accepted Timothy, who fit, age-wise, right in the middle of their family. I often wonder what this child must have been thinking in coming to a strange home, having many memories of his parents which caused him great pain, wondering whether this new family was really going to like him and wishing that he could be with his brothers and sisters. But his adopted family were people who could sit and listen to his recollections, could cope with his fears and anxiety, could allow him to adjust very slowly to their family and could accept with satisfaction his level of attainment. Timothy has been in that home long enough so that we know he has really accepted these people as his family. He had never been to Sunday School before in his life, and he is now attending a Bible-believing church and a Christian day school. The change in his environment will greatly affect his future. I believe those adoptive parents are being used by the Lord just as surely as any pastor or missionary is used in God's service.

Yes, it takes some special characteristics in a couple who accept an older child. They must be especially flexible in their willingness and ability to cope with individual behavior—behavior which they may not condone. They must also be sensitive to the emotional needs of the older child who has been traumatized by circumstances. They must try to understand the causes of his behavior and be able to talk with him about his attitudes, feelings, fears and expectations.

13 / Delights and Dilemmas in Caring for the Fatherless

Doris Wheeler

God has enjoined us in Exodus 22 and 23 to care for the widows and fatherless. He repeats this injunction in James 1:27 where He states that pure religion is to visit the widows and fatherless in their affliction. Have you ever stopped to think that there are many ways to be fatherless? One can be fatherless because his father has died, is away in prison or has abandoned the family. Again, a child may be fatherless because there has been separation or divorce between his parents or because father, who lives in the home, is not taking any responsibility as a father. At the Evangelical Child and Family Agency we are caring for children in all of these categories. Thus the families that work with us are involved in caring for the fatherless as God commanded. I'd like to share some of their delights and dilemmas with you, both to encourage those of you who have not yet taken in a "chosen" child and also those of you who have.

I think first of four children who have been in our care for a number of years. Their father committed suicide soon after they were placed in one of our foster homes.

Several months later their mother was killed in a tragic car accident. It was not an easy task for these foster parents to help the children through their grief.

I can hear the words of another foster mother who, with her husband, recently accepted three little children, all under age six. These children are fatherless because dad is in prison and will not be coming home very soon. Mother died of cancer three days after the children came to us. The foster mother called the agency, asking that we either take one of the children or give some kind of relief. It was one of those days when the youngest boy had all the pots and pans on the floor, the middle boy had just torn his new suit and the oldest boy didn't want to go to school.

This foster mother had to learn that she needn't be perfect. She could not overextend herself and still have enough emotional energy to meet the daily crises. Therefore, some of the housework must be left undone, a meal or two each week came from McDonalds or "the Colonel" and one outside activity had to go. God was showing her how to accept herself with her human limitations.

One of the disappointing things for these parents is that love is not always returned. A child often is not ready to give himself emotionally to a new set of parents. This comes from being hurt through prior separation and not wanting to be hurt again. Sometimes parents have to love and love and love, receiving very little in return.

One of our little foster girls, for instance, waits anxiously at the window for her foster daddy to come home because she wants to be with him so badly. Yet, when he comes through the door, she runs to the bedroom and hides under the bed, really fearing to get too close to him. She has been in the home for some months now and this behavior is beginning to change but her ambivalence is certainly demonstrated in this behavior.

Another disappointment that sometimes comes to adoptive parents is the development of behavior problems in the children—not necessarily because they are adopted but because they are human. I have had a number of adoptive couples come to me in deep distress because their young teenage children were following patterns not in keeping with their parents' desires. In fact, some of the behavior has been very unacceptable: truancy from school, difficulty with the law, use of drugs, sexual deviance, etc. The fact is that adopted children have severe problems, as do many "natural" children. I believe this is especially disappointing to adoptive parents since they have chosen to take the responsibility and want so much to "do a good job with the child."

Recently an adoptive couple shared with me that their daughter will hardly speak to them and that she is keeping company with peers who are a very poor influence on her. Another couple were having similar problems with their son. Counseling is, of course, suggested and the parents and child are up-held in prayer. But often parents have to give the child to the Lord's keeping while they wait prayerfully for a change in behavior.

The existence of the natural parent often provokes anxiety. Sometimes the adoptive or foster child will throw this in the face of the couple saying, "My mother would let me do this," or, "If I was with my mother she would understand." This is a situation which must be reckoned with in the adoptive or foster home. Yet, many children at one time or another say to their parents, "If I belonged to the neighbors, it would be better." This problem is not peculiar to the adoptive or foster situation. But it does upset parents who hear it too often or at the wrong times.

Also, there is an uneasiness on the part of the adoptive parents that the natural parent may return and request the child. Though this happens rarely, it is an increasing issue in the media and there are occasions when a child (usually an infant) is returned to the natural parent.

Lineage is important with many adopted children. A teenage child will usually want to know as much about his "birth" parents as he can. For this reason, our agency gives the adoptive parents as much background information as possible, including personality, talents and physical description of the natural parents, so that they share this with the adopted child. In the future adoption files will probably be more easily accessible to the adoptive person. There are many positive values in this.

A fifteen year old boy whom we had placed was exhibiting very anti-social behavior and wanting very much to see his natural mother. The adoptive parents and this boy came to us for counseling. Together we decided that, if we could find the natural mother and obtain her permission it would be a good thing for the boy to meet her. We located the natural mother who was willing to see him.

A meeting was set up in our office and the mother and son had a very rewarding visit. The boy had no desire to leave his adoptive home nor did he request further visits with his natural mother. His behavior improved steadily from that point on—apparently an insatiable desire to know his origin had been fulfilled.

Many such positive accounts can be given of meetings with natural parents. Of course, there are some visits which have not gone so well. This constitutes a dilemma for adoptive parents. But in those few cases where contact might actually be made it can be a very helpful and positive experience for all concerned.

Another difficult area is the extra medical and educational needs which must be met with some "chosen children." A couple of years ago we placed a little girl whom we knew would need three major operations within a year after placement. It was not known how normal a life this little girl would lead and so we needed a family who could accept her with her limitations and with all the time, energy and money it was going to take to meet her physical needs. This particular little girl has recovered very well and is leading an almost normal life. She has been a delight for her adoptive parents. But it was not always easy having to go to the clinic two or three times a week and learning to give some home nursing care. It was not always easy to bear the anxiety of a long and dangerous surgical procedure. This couple had not chosen an easy way.

But as we remember some of the rough spots we also remember some of the joys. There is the little foster girl who, at the age of seven, came into the care of our agency. She was placed in a modest Christian home, but to this little girl it was like heaven. I'll never forget what she told her foster mother the morning after she arrived. In her little childish way she said, "Boy, it sure was great to sleep all night and not worry about the rats running over you."

A teenage girl in one of our foster homes recently won a trophy for her willingness and ability to share Christ with others. That is satisfaction. Then we have a little four-year-old foster boy who cannot stay with his natural mother because of her instability and drunkenness. This little fellow was riding along with one of our workers and broke into song . . . "Jesus loves me, this I know. . . ."

What an assurance for him, what a joy for us!

Then there is the little nine-year-old foster boy who, though mentally limited and functioning at a preschool level, is full of energy. On his first day in the new foster home he bounded upstairs and emptied all of the dresser drawers. From there he went to the closets and "rearranged" the contents. Yes, some of this was hyper-activity and some of it was fear. The foster mother had many days of exhaustion, discouragement and frustration. Little Allen could not put his clothes on right, could not button his sweater and invariably could not work the zipper. And then one day he put his clothes on in the right direction and he buttoned the sweater! What a rewarding day! Almost everyone in the neighborhood heard about this victory. It was a real success for this little guy and a great satisfaction for the foster parents who love him and are trying so hard.

These ups and downs, these disappointments and thrills, are complicated by issues somewhat exaggerated in adoptive and foster parents. One is the matter of discipline. It seems to be a bit more difficult for "chosen parents" to discipline consistently. This seems to come from a slight pity for the child or from an over-cautious attitude. Fear of being disliked by the child is also a factor.

Overprotection is also common, especially with a first adopted child. This attitude is characterized by parents who think, "We have accepted this child and now must treat him like a china doll." Contributing to the overprotective response is the fact that many couples have waited years for a child, sometimes having lost several through miscarriage or death. Now that they have a child they overprotect through fear of another loss.

Unrealistic expectations plague some families. If the

expectations are too high for the individual child, disappointment will follow. In fact, the dangers are even greater: the child may feel rejected or worthless because he senses the parents' disapproval. This can then lead to many forms of personality dysfunction.

Guilt or fear of failure are other feelings that enter this special parenthood. Some adoptive parents feel that "someone else might have done a better job with this child" or "it's not his fault that he has us for parents, therefore, we must do a very good job." Though these feelings are unrealistic, nevertheless they are often part of the thought process with adoptive or foster parents.

Adoptive and foster parenthood has its special delights, dilemmas and pitfalls. We shouldn't be surprised to find it a dynamic, exciting and sometimes turbulent growth experience.

About the Contributors

Diny Bailey was born in Holland and spent her childhood there during the war. She came to America after high school. Altogether, she and her husband have taken in over 20 foster children. She attends Grace Baptist Church in Lombard and enjoys sewing, knitting, and swimming.

Lane T. Dennis lives with his wife Ebeth and their four children in Wheaton, Illinois. An ordained minister, Rev. Dennis is the managing editor for Good News Publishers. He is the author of *A Reason for Hope* and numerous articles in Christian periodicals. He has received the M.Div. from McCormick Theological Seminary and is a candidate for the Ph.D. from Northwestern University. The Dennises enjoy many outdoor family activities. Before returning to Wheaton, they lived in Europe and the American North Woods.

Muriel B. Dennis is President of Good News Publishers which she co-founded with her late husband, Clyde H. Dennis. She is a charter member of Evangelical Christian

Publisher's Association and served as a board member and as secretary. Director of literature ministries in Switzerland and Northern Nigeria and involved with literature outreach in Europe, South America, Africa, Indonesia, the Middle East, Ireland and Asia, she represented the press at the World Congress on Evangelism in Lausanne and the National Religious Broadcaster's Association convention. She has three children and 10 grandchildren.

JoAnn Harvey is a graduate of Pasadena College and Biola. Her husband, the Rev. Robert Harvey, graduated from Occidental College and Fuller Theological Seminary, and is currently Pastor of Bethel Orthodox Presbyterian Church in Wheaton, Illinois. With their two children, the Harveys enjoy traveling and family sports.

Judy Johnson is a retired registered nurse and is married to a civil engineer. They have two children, ages 15 and 11. She and her husband enjoy horseback riding and water skiing. The whole family is active in their church fellowship.

Ted Johnson, with his wife Gerri and their two children, Jeff (17) and Jill (14), lives in St. Anthony Village, Minnesota. He travels throughout Minnesota and Wisconsin as a sales representative for a wholesale building materials firm. He and Gerri are members of Salem Covenant Church. They enjoy spending as much time as possible with their family at their lake home in Northern Minnesota.

C. Everett Koop is the Surgeon-in-Chief of the Children's Hospital of Philadelphia and Professor of Pediatric Surgery at the University of Pennsylvania. A graduate of Dartmouth College, he received his medical degree from Cornell and a Doctor of Science from Pennsylvania. He is the founding editor of the *Journal of Pediatric Surgery,* an Elder of the Tenth Presyterian Church in Philadelphia, and the father of four children and a foster child.

Carolyn Nystrom is a graduate of Wheaton College. She taught for ten years in the public schools. She and her husband Roger have four children and occasionally add foster children to their brood. Carolyn enjoys music, gardening and small group inductive Bible studies. She is the author of numerous books and articles including the Moody Press book *Forgive Me if I'm Frayed Around the Edges* which recounts Randy's beginnings in the Nystrom family.

Dale Evans Rogers is the author of 17 books, including *Angel Unawares,* and over 100 popular songs. The wife of "The King of the Cowboys," Roy Rogers, she is a film, television and rodeo star in her own right. She recently received an honorary doctorate from Bethany College in West Virginia. Roy and Dale have nine children—four of them adopted—16 grandchildren and two great-grandchildren.

Bonnie Wheeler uses her interests in interior decorating, needlework and indoor gardening to create a cheerful home for her husband, Dennis and their six children (three "homemade" and three adopted). Dennis is Sunday School superintendent at Fremont Neighborhood Church; Bonnie has been on "leave of absence" from her church activities since the arrival of Alicia. She tries to make time each day for her free-lance writing and has sold to *Moody Monthly, Daily Blesings, Family Life Today* and *The Aliance Witness*. She is currently working on a book.

Doris Wheeler has been the Executive Director of the Evangelical Child and Family Agency for the past five and one-half years. For five years prior she was Director of Social Services at this agency. In all, she has had 14 years' experience as a graduate social worker. A registered nurse, Miss Wheeler has the BS from Wheaton College and the MSW from the University of Chicago. Out of a deep concern for spiritual values as well as family life, she has visited mission fields and participated as a counselor in evangelistic crusades. These experiences enhance her service to the Chicago community in the field of child welfare.